Introduction

 WHILE VOLUMES HAVE been written about Britain's country houses, their grand history, architecture, art and gardens, and the power and frivolity that governed them, a strange veil of silence seems to have been drawn over them during the period 1939–45, a major watershed in the country's history, when these houses made a contribution to the war effort that seems far more worthy of chronicling than some of the glamorous hunting and shooting years prior to the Second World War. The damaging effects of the war have been examined in the light of the destruction and demolition that ensued after 1945, but little has been mentioned about the wartime role of these houses, which proved invaluable in preserving human lives, in providing retreats for the wounded or dispossessed, and in conserving the nation's treasures.

The number of country houses in Great Britain is uncountable, since there is no clear definition of what a country house is. How big? How much land? How far from town? As a benchmark, Hugh Montgomery-Massingberd, editor of *Burke's and Saville's Guide to Country Houses*, estimates that perhaps 10,000 country seats would have to be included in order to make his volume comprehensive.

There is no way this book could cover so many houses, even though it is likely that a large percentage of them played some sort of role in World War Two. I have simply chosen those with unusually interesting or poignant stories to tell, those possessing particularly thorough archives of the period, or those whose wartime experiences seem typical of a great number of other houses across the country. Many people who lived through that time will have other stories to tell, of other houses, other requisitions. There is much more material than I could hope to cover. My goal was somehow to contain my research in such a way that would touch on as many aspects of the subject as possible without omissions or repetition.

As a war baby, brought up not to talk about the war or my family's experiences in it (an uncle killed in Africa, another incarcerated in a Japanese prison camp), I was struck most forcibly in working on this book by the astonishing bravery of all those who stayed at home, living in the country, making do, in circumstances quite unlike any they could ever have dreamed of. While much has been written about the military aspects of the war, and about the terrible toll exacted upon the major cities of Britain, there has been a modest silence about the endurance and resourcefulness of people (mostly women) who lived in dark, chilly isolation most of those six years – women born to privilege and comfort, accustomed to being waited on and admired, who had almost overnight either to move out of their ancient homes or to decamp to out-of-the-way quarters while strangers took over their drawing rooms and bedrooms.

Even under the best of circumstances, there is a sense of violation in the act of opening one's home to others, as all those who have lent or let their houses know. For some disenfranchised house-owners, the challenge was to maintain tolerable living standards for families and friends as long as the war lasted. With their houses taken over by others, the younger women or those unfettered with children could either work with the new tenants (as hospital commandant or estate manager, for instance), or hire themselves out in an entirely new capacity. Sheltered, untrained as they were, many jumped at the opportunity to make something different out of their lives. Throwing off their conventional roles of *noblesse oblige*, they took on jobs that contributed in a major way to the war effort. The feeling of exhilaration this inspired can still be heard in their voices as they recollect, often almost wistfully, those exceptional, aberrant, heady years.

While the war brought many of its participants rudely into the twentieth century, particularly those who for so many centuries had hidden behind the porticoes and pillars of class superiority, it also gave that class a human face. There are many stories of evacuee children returning to the houses they lived in during those years, and of servicemen writing letters of gratitude to the owners of houses in which they were billeted. Many houses (including The Hazells, Chatsworth, Blenheim, Castle Howard, Knebworth and Deene Park mentioned in this book) hold reunions to commemorate friends and colleagues who became connected in such an unlikely manner so many years ago. In the larger context of the social and architectural life of the British country house, with which we are by now so familiar, 1939–45 is a very little blip on the screen of time. But those six years of history made an indelible mark on these houses, as these living witnesses still meet to testify.

This book is divided into two sections. The first part, 'The Country', describes the general conditions under which people in the country lived during 1939–45, and the various forms of requisitioning that took place. The second part, 'The Houses', examines in detail the experiences of individual houses occupied under the various headings of School, Military Billet, Hospital, Treasure Repository and Secret Operations. In this way each house is given a context, and the personal stories are placed in their proper setting, relating them to the overriding circumstances of wartime living.

THE
COUNTRY

The Call-up

'To the owner and occupier of the land and buildings described in the schedule hereto annexed. I, Colonel John Doe, being one of a class of persons to whom the Secretary of State as a competent authority for the purposes of Part IV of the Defence Regulations, 1939, has in exercise of the powers contained in That Part of the said Defence Regulations delegated the necessary authority, give notice that I, on behalf of the Secretary of State take possession of the land and buildings described in the schedule hereby annexed.'

 THIS FORM, LANDING on your plate at breakfast time, would probably have rather ruined the taste of the bacon and eggs that morning. It was with this order, or a local one like it, that in the autumn of 1939 owners of country houses regarded as potentially useful in the war effort were informed of the loss of their properties to the Government. Requisitioning in wartime was of course a familiar course of action for any country involved in hostilities. Some houses had already played their part in the First World War, mostly as hospitals in that war of so many human casualties. Others were being called up for the first time, and although most house-owners knew the inevitable summons would arrive, they were little prepared for the upheavals that would ensue.

Nor did the Government itself seem very well-prepared. The first task was to make a central register of properties throughout the country, listing size, location, suitability, etc. But while government plans for requisitioning began in the mid 1930s, by the beginning of 1939 no official register of houses had been drawn up. There seems to have been much jockeying for position, not only from the various government departments, but also from the house-owners, this bureaucratic in-fighting preventing an organized effort at drawing up a comprehensive list.

Before war had been declared, Whitehall's first priority for requisitioning was to prepare for the evacuation of people (and in particular, children) from war-vulnerable areas. On 9 February 1939, Sir Thomas Moore asked in the House of Lords whether any survey had been made of 'empty mansions and other suitable empty properties throughout the country for purposes of evacuation'. The answer was no, and local authorities were requested to complete such surveys by the end of the month.

Naturally enough, house-owners were not enthused by the idea of hordes of working-class children invading their homes unnecessarily. But the sensitive issue of who got possession of what houses was being equally hotly contested by competing government offices. On 18 February 1939, E. N. de Normann at the Office of Works wrote to A. N. Rucker at the Ministry of Health:

'I am unhappy as to the possibility of large country houses in all our evacuation districts being included in the accommodation for civilian refugees.

'As you know we have only earmarked accommodation for government staffs. If there were a move of government to these districts we should be faced at once with requests to provide accommodation for all sorts of other users: Royalty, Court officials, Foreign embassies, Parliamentary officials, essential nuclei of financial and commercial houses who must keep in touch with the government. In addition we may have to run hostels; in short, there are a thousand and one possibilities and I have always looked to these large country houses in the Government evacuation districts as supplying us at any rate with a minimum of essential accommodation. If you agree with me, what is the best way from the point of view of the Ministry of seeing that these houses are not brought into the refugee picture?'

Mr Rucker diplomatically replied, 'The large country houses to which you refer must inevitably be included in the surveys made by local authorities. It would be impossible to leave such houses out of account on the chance that you would want them, and questions would almost certainly be asked why they were omitted, but if and when you can tell us that you are interested in such country houses, there will be no difficulty in ensuring that no one is actually sent to these houses under the evacuation scheme.'

This inter-departmental bickering seems to have inhibited more practical action. As late as March 1939, Lord Middleton tabled a question in the House of Lords asking H. M. Government if they had yet scheduled large houses in rural areas for special purposes in the event of a national emergency. Ministry of Health officials attempted to get him to withdraw the question, on the grounds that 'the possible use of large houses that may be scheduled is a very secret matter and it would be definitely contrary to the public interest for the matter to be debated.' The MOH believed that secrecy was essential to the success of their evacuation operations, and questions such as Lord Middleton's threatened their plans and put pressure on them to come out into the open.

But Lord Middleton's question would also have revealed the embarrassing fact that an official register of houses had still not been completed. The prospect of cataloguing every large country house in Britain with a view to its prospective wartime use was, to be sure, a task to test the workings of the most advanced civil service machinery. But without such a list, the requisitioning of houses remained an arbitrary and chaotic affair.

Under pressure, Lord Middleton agreed to withdraw his question. In fact, His Lordship's main motive was not to embarrass the Government. He merely hoped to find out if his own house might be scheduled, so that 'he could be recruiting the necessary voluntary labour in the neighbourhood, by having whatever drills were necessary and so on.' While the Government continued to procrastinate, house-owners were marshalling rather more organized forces to attempt to rationalize the requisitioning process. The Earl of Beauchamp drew up a memo, for instance, presumably after discussion with his peers, which was circulated to the Ministry of Health, the Office of Works, and the War Office. It covers almost every possible angle of requisitioning, from the point of view, of course, of the owners. It reads, in part, as follows:

LARGE HOUSES IN WAR TIME

Everyone will agree that:—
1 Large houses have played an important part in history.
2 Many of them beautify the countryside.
3 Most of them should be preserved for ever, but
4 In a national emergency, they must be made the best possible use of, like everyone and everything else.
   The Government should examine this question very thoroughly.
5 There seem to be four ways in which large houses could be used:—
   a As hospitals, civil, or for the forces of the Crown.
   b Accommodation for refugee children or adults.
   c Accommodation for the forces of the Crown.
   d Storage of pictures, or other records of national importance.
6 The large houses used must be structurally sound, and unless used for

storage only should be equipped with adequate A. water supply system, B. drainage, C. light and power, or gas. Otherwise they will not be of much use.

Lord Beauchamp urged that the Government complete a register of all big houses and their particulars, so that in an emergency immediate steps could be taken to prepare the selected houses for their pre-arranged functions, thus saving valuable time. 'In these circumstances,' he pointed out, 'the only problems for the owner of a large house would be to get his furniture stored away. Normally, this could be done in a day or two, but in a national emergency, no one knows how long it would take. Therefore, if possible, assistance should be given so that the householder in an emergency could get this done as soon as possible.'

Lord Beauchamp gave as an example his own house, Madresfield Court, in Great Malvern, Worcestershire. 'My home is on the big side,' he conceded, 'although not as large as some. It has about a hundred rooms, of which sixty-four are bedrooms.' Lord Beauchamp announced that the War Office had accepted Madresfield as a hospital, 'and have put it on a register kept by the Office of Works, who will presumably communicate with me if necessary.' ('I would like to know,' he added, 'why the Office of Works and not the War Office keeps this register.')

The end of His Lordship's memo sounded a ringing note of patriotism. 'If the question of the use of large houses is dealt with on the above lines, I am sure that most of the owners will cooperate in any way they can, and if a war does occur, it may very well be that the large houses of this country will play a more important part than they have ever played before in our national history.'

The effect of this memo on the government offices was salutary. A letter to the Earl from T. A. G. Charlton of the War Office hastily assured His Lordship that 'If it becomes necessary to use Madresfield Court in the event of an emergency you will hear from us and not from the Office of Works.' Mr Charlton also said, 'I might add that if you are in a position to persuade owners of large houses to offer their homes in an emergency for any national purposes ... such offers would be of value in helping to settle a problem of considerable magnitude.'

By May 1939 a Central Register of Accommodation was finally in circulation. Its effectiveness was somewhat diminished by not being complete due to delays by local councils, organizations etc., in compiling and submitting their sections, as well as by the fact that the Register was still being treated as 'strictly confidential' even after the war began. However, an average of 50 complete sets were distributed to local authorities, chief constables, estate surveyors, and so on. Fifty thousand extra pages of addenda were distributed each week. In fact, so many pages were being added that on one occasion the current weekly addendum comprised 721 pages and weighed 9 lbs, at which point some bright clerk suggested that the sets currently sent to the various heads of the War Office, Admiralty, Air Ministry, Ministry of Transport, Ministry of Education, Ministry of Health, etc., be cancelled to save paper.

The Register listed the name and address of the property, the local authority, a description of the premises, proposed user of the premises, stage of emergency at which premises were to be taken over, for how long, and which department was to occupy them. All this was compiled in the utmost secrecy. An undated, unsigned memo from the Ministry of Works categorically declared: 'Though premises are earmarked for requisition and placed on the Central Register with the Office of Works, the owner of the property is not to be informed that this has been done. Nor is it the intention that he should be so informed or find out since circumstances are constantly changing, both as regards the condition of the property, the military requirements and degree and state of emergency.'

The memo-writer then concedes that, 'though it is undesirable to tie the hands of the War Department it is not the intention to inflict undue hardship on owners of property or to deprive them of a reasonable degree of personal accommodation, unless and until they are able to make alternative arrangements for their own accommodation.'

While house-owners were supposed to be in the dark, some of them, at least, knew perfectly well what was being plotted in Whitehall. The prospects raised by Lord Beauchamp's list – hospital, refugee accommodation, military billet, repository for national treasures – must have haunted the imaginations of many a country squire in those months before war was declared. Would you rather have nurses or schoolchildren swarming over your heirloom furniture and rugs? Which would you prefer, corporals or Caravaggios? Some owners jumped the gun, so to speak, by offering their houses before they were commandeered, therefore ensuring a better class of occupation. All over the country, discreet letters and phone calls were sent to prospective institutions, in hopes of circumventing the nightmarish prospects of army, air force, or other evacuee groups forced upon them by the war bureaucracies. Thus the present Duchess of Devonshire relates that when he saw that war was inevitable, the 10th Duke made an arrangement for Penrhos College, a girls' public school, to move to Chatsworth, 'realising that a girls' school would make far better tenants than soldiers'. The owner of Elton Hall, bachelor Granville

Proby, went one stage further. During a discussion as to whether Elton should become a girls' school or a repository for works of art, Mr Proby is said to have declared, 'I think we ought to have the Old Masters. After all we do know that girls can be produced at any time by processes of nature; but Old Masters are quite irreplaceable.' In this case the preemptive ruse did not work. Elton Hall became a hospital, as it had been in World War One.

While some owners had greatness thrust upon them, others were all too eager to pursue it. Requisitioning was rightly seen by some as a saving of run-down or economically ruinous houses. Mrs Violet Van der Elst, for instance, could not really afford to keep up Harlaxton House in Lincolnshire. What better than for her to offer it to the War Office for use by the First Airborne Division? Other owners wrote letters to the Office of Works offering their houses for more patriotic reasons. There was a Miss Nasmyth, of Glenfarg House in Scotland, for instance, who offered her mansion as a convalescent home, as long as she could collect from the orchard as much fruit as she required. Other conditions set forth by her more fastidious solicitors included space for Miss Nasmyth's 'old servant', payment for coal, anthracite and the telephone bill, and the requirement that if the officers and medical staff utilized shooting privileges on the estate, 'they will be required to do so in a fair and sportsmanlike manner, and Miss Nasmyth has expressed the wish that should any reasonable quantity of game be killed a little might be sent her.' Some patriots were spinsters, some old men, like Francis Fane, of Wormsley Park, Watlington, Oxfordshire, who offered his house for the storage of government papers in early 1940. 'I suppose I am too old for you to make use of my services now,' he added wistfully. (He was over seventy.) The man from the Ministry thought this house eminently suitable, and reported that Mr Fane would be willing to act as keeper if required. 'He seems to have had some experience of this during the last war.'

Some owners made requisitioning final and sold their houses, perhaps seeing the dismal future for large country houses after the war. Listings in the glossy magazines of properties for sale swelled after 1939, with prices that now seem inconceivable – a Georgian manor house near Winchester offered at £2,500, a six-bedroom house on the Thames with an acre of land, £5,000. The very large country mansions that could be useful to institutions brought higher prices, of course. John G. Murray sold Wrest Park, Bedfordshire, for £25,000 in 1939 to the Sun Insurance Company, who, in anticipation of war, promptly moved there from London.

Lord Astor offered Cliveden to the Government and received 83 child evacuees during the first week of the war. But in the First World War Cliveden had been a Canadian hospital and it was rapidly apparent that it was in this role that the house was most urgently needed in the Second World War. The problem of hospital accommodation became acute almost immediately, as heavy early casualties made great demands on the houses already requisitioned, and space, suitable heating, plumbing and electrical services were all at a premium. In 1940, the Emergency Hospital Scheme urgently called for greatly increased house-requisitioning, leading as usual to heightened tension between the various war departments.

In July 1940, Sir Alfred Webb-Johnson, Chairman of the Red Cross, wrote to Sir George Christal at the MOH about the bewilderment and confusion suffered by house-owners because of these internecine conflicts. 'I think this is partly due to ... two sets of people inspecting their houses – your Regional Officers to see if they are suitable for regional hospitals, and our County Representative to see if they are suitable for convalescent homes.' Meanwhile in August, the Deputy Director of Hospitals, Hyw Wells, lamented to the War Office: 'We often find ourselves in conflict with the local military authorities. Although I fully appreciate that under normal circumstances we must give way to the requirements of the military there are, I feel, certain occasions when a house which is particularly suitable for hospital purposes is taken by the military authorities although there may be another house nearby suitable for billeting and not suitable for a hospital ... One such case at the moment, Tyringham House, Newport Pagnell, Bucks ...'

This complaint apparently hit home, for later in 1940 a number of houses were relinquished by the War Office to the Red Cross, including Rystock House, Exmouth, Shuckburgh, Daventry, Dunraven Castle, Glamorgan, Winkfield Place, Windsor, Wargrave and Deanwood in Berkshire, Bigham Abbey, Bucks, and Irton Hall, Cambridgeshire. Almost 3,000 large country houses were requisitioned by the Ministry of Health alone.

While requisitioning in many cases saved the more precariously-maintained houses from economic and structural ruin, by 1941 some of the patriotic fervour of the house-owners had dimmed. In many cases the realities of requisition were very painful. Orders were often given in a high-handed and inconsiderate way; the best buildings were requisitioned by government staffs when less attractive accommodation could have been acquired with less personal hardship or loss; houses were requisitioned and vacated, only to be left unoccupied. In many cases, the elderly were asked to move out of houses they had lived in for all their lives, while hordes of strangers moved in. Families were split, people suddenly found themselves alone and helpless. Lady Braybrooke, for instance, was about to move into Heydon Rectory, Cambridgeshire, to supervise the settlement of her late husband's estate at Audley End. Instead she found herself homeless when the Rectory itself was requisitioned. The Popes, an elderly Major and his wife, were asked to vacate Ashwick Hall, in Wiltshire, within fourteen days. Major Pope was a sick man. His London house had been taken over by the Government and its furniture stored at Ashwick. His only choice was the alternative of staying in eight rooms in the house, entirely inadequate space for his family of children, grandchildren and nurses. The McDougalls of Aubrey House, in Berkshire, moved out in December 1940 to accommodate a group of RAF officers. The RAF left in 1941 so the McDougalls moved back in, only to be asked by the authorities to move out again later that year.

One of the more eccentric stories of the requisition period of the war concerns a piece of the Bentley Manor Estate, Stanmore, Middlesex, most of which, including Bentley Priory, was already owned by the Air Ministry. A Mrs L'Anson-Anson offered to sell her part of this property to the Air Ministry in 1936. Negotiations ensued in a rather vague manner, and in 1939 the site was requisitioned by an Army anti-aircraft Brigade. Mrs Anson was furious and claimed she had almost sold the property and stood to lose over £10,000. She complained of 'theft of her property' and launched a postal attack that would have impressed even Bomber Command: fifteen letters to the Air Ministry, five letters to Neville Chamberlain, three letters to Winston Churchill, letters to the H. M. the King (delivered personally to the Palace), the Home Secretary, Duff Cooper, Clement Attlee, Sir Archibald Sinclair, President Roosevelt, Mr Menzies, and an anonymous letter to King George at Buckingham Palace. Included with her letters were extracts from newspapers about dog-breeding and amateur plans of the property, plus accusations that the Air Ministry were conducting Gestapo methods against a poor widow. The King also found enclosed a picture of the Lass of Richmond Hill, a supposed ancestress.

An official of the Air Ministry succinctly summed it up: 'The plain facts are that this lady has in recent years speculated with her property by enlarging Bentley Manor and has got herself into financial difficulties from which she hopes to be extricated by payments from the Air Ministry.'

While fending off the more erratic candidates for requisitioning, the Ministries began to take note of the increasing complaints they received about the procedure itself. In November 1941, instructions were sent out that 'local authorities should, so far as practicable, make a periodic review of future requirements so as to give owners and occupiers of property the longest possible notice of the intention to requisition.' By 1943, the Air Ministry was also expressing concern about the damage that had been caused to requisitioned properties and their contents after they were vacated by the occupying units. 'Such damage has been suffered not only by RAF property but also by the furniture and effects of the owners of premises which have been stored therein and for those whose safe custody the RAF is responsible.'

The RAF, of course, was not the only culprit. The exigencies of war and the continuing billet and hospital emergencies meant that there was little time for courtesy and consideration, even less time to give adequate notice, and house-owners simply had to make the best of it. An added burden to the already strained requisitioning system was the entry into the war of the Americans. Between 1940 and 1945 almost half a million foreign troops were stationed in Britain, rising to one and a half million at the time of the Normandy landings. All these people had to eat and sleep somewhere.

This chaotic situation meant that where alert land-agents or family solicitors were involved, an owner might get a contract of requisition and compensation that was legal and binding. But in other cases, an inadequate agreement was often hastily cobbled together to fit the emergency requirements – compensation remaining one of the thorniest issues of all for those who endured the necessary torment of requisition. While various Acts of Parliament such as the Compensation (Defence) Act of 1939 and the War Damage Act of 1941 purported to deal with damage to institutions or private houses, most agreements were made in haste with the entering troops, issued sometimes merely in handwritten guarantees from the commanding officer. It will be seen that one of the most difficult aspects of the post-war period for country houses was the lack of proper rights to claim for damage, and while nobody was surprised at the intractability of the problem, it added an extra economic burden to people who could little afford it.

Very few houses, whatever their size or fame, escaped requisitioning in some form or other. Some had already been turned over to military use, such as Bletchley Park, which had been bought by the Government between the wars to house its Codes and Cyphers School and was occupied by this organization when war broke out in 1939; or Bentley Priory, which had become the Headquarters of the newly-formed Fighter Command in 1936, and in whose Ops Room Churchill spent the decisive days of the Battle of Britain. Churchill also requisitioned, if that is not too strong a word, Ronald Tree's house in Oxfordshire, Ditchley Park, as a place to spend weekends 'when the moon is high'. This was Churchill's own typically rhetorical phrase, meaning that German reconnaissance planes had flown over Chequers, the Prime Minister's official country residence, after the war started, taking photographs of the house and its surroundings, and there was some anxiety that in good night-flying weather there might be an attack on the country's leader. (Ditchley had already taken in a nursery school, evacuated from the East End of London, as well as other evacuees from the same slum area, who, as Ronald Tree observed, were 'not encouraged to be very clean in their habits', and soon went back to London. The nursery school, however, stayed at Ditchley for a year.)

Some houses were given special treatment because of their unusually rare or historical interiors, such as Wilton House, which was used for strategic planning purposes. (Presumably even the Government flinched at the thought of a regiment at play in the Double Cube Room.) A few were rejected because of impracticality, such as Felbrigg Hall in Norfolk, which had no electricity at all! But even if the house was rejected, parkland was always useful, and hardly an acre of the British countryside was not ultimately recruited for war service. Even park railings were summarily removed for scrap.

In *The Valley of Bones*, Anthony Powell describes his battalion's occupation of Castlemallock, a vast, inconvenient castle in Northern Ireland that had lain untenanted for twenty or thirty years before its requisitioning. 'There was an undoubted aptness in this sham fortress, monument to a tasteless, half-baked romanticism, becoming now, in truth, a military stronghold, its stone walls and vaulted ceilings echoing at last to the clatter of arms and oaths of soldiery.' Many English houses found themselves also once again fulfilling the role for which they had originally been built – as fortresses against marauding invaders. The fear of invasion was as real in 1940 as it had been in medieval times, and the houses were called upon once again, as Lord Beauchamp had predicted, to serve their country's cause.

Packing the Silver

IT WAS AS MUCH the practical requirements of requisitioning as anything else that forced country house-owners to commit themselves to the realities of war. While the feeling expressed in movies and writings of the time seems to have been the familiar British-export attitude of 'Here we go, chaps,' for those living in houses which had seen the heyday of Edwardian grandeur and had survived the decimations of the First World War, the sense of falling off the edge of a cliff was strongly in evidence. Many memoirs of the period express the feeling of nostalgia and finality recorded by the late Lord Egremont in this description of a dinner held with his uncle Lord Leconfield at Petworth on the eve of the Second World War:

'The golden candelabra are throwing a glittering light on the Paul Storr gold and silver plate, the Monteith bowls, the silver wine-coolers on the side-tables, the rococo pier-glasses . . . In the background were the footmen in their blue Wyndham livery with their silver-crested buttons agleam . . .'

Julian Fane evokes the same sense of dislocation or doomsday, describing a 'last' dinner party just after the war had started, with some visiting cavalry officers at the family house, Lyegrove:

'The silver candelabra with the red paper shades singed in places by the flames of candles were spaced along the length of the oak refectory table. My mother sat at one end and my father at the other – and my sisters glittered and flirted in between. The five or six guests were flushed not just with military fitness by now, also with food and wine . . . It was impressively romantic and traditional. It might have been a painting entitled: Nobleman Entertains Soldiery Before the Battle – it was like the Duchess of Richmond's Waterloo Ball on a small scale.'

Fane adds grimly that two of the men who sat down to dinner were later killed, and his father, the Earl of Westmorland, did not have very long to live.

What was to become of the candelabra, the Paul Storr gold and silver plate, the Monteith bowls, the rococo pier-glasses? What was to happen to the oak refectory table, to the liveried footmen and their gleaming buttons, to Lyegrove itself? Up and down the country people were asking similar questions. 'Princess Marie Louise,' reported *The Tatler*, 'who is a very practical person, helped Lady Beauchamp in the packing up of some of the family treasures, such as the collection of snuffboxes and so forth, which are being cleared away in readiness for the moment when hospital equipment will take the place of the lovely things which fill every nook and corner . . .'

For some, declaration of war produced the kind of apocalyptic mood that gripped Chips Channon, for instance, who rushed down to Kelvedon, his country house in Essex, that fateful September weekend:

'I went to Kelvedon on Saturday afternoon in lovely weather in the hope of a peaceful perfect Sunday, but it was not to be. There were endless decisions to be made; papers to be stored; fuss and confusion; irritated servants; neglected dogs; plate-room and cellar complications. We packed up all our jewelled toys, the Fabergé bibelots and gold watches, etc., and counted the wine, then we welcomed 150 refugees, all nice East End people, but . . . our Sunday was not as happy as I had hoped.'

Burying things was one solution. In 1940, Alan Turing, the brilliant mathematician and code-breaker, buried two silver ingots in the woods behind Bletchley as a hedge against inflation, and Chips Channon buried two tin boxes containing his diaries and the aforementioned jewelled toys and bibelots in the village churchyard, as a hedge against dispossession. 'Mortimer, who dug the hole, is discreet, and he waited until all the gardeners had gone home; we watched the earth cover them over; may they sleep in peace. Mother Earth must hold many other such secrets in her bosom.'

As the requisition orders came through, house-owners were faced with the task of somehow protecting centuries-old panelling, mouldings, paintings, porcelain, furniture, furnishings and rugs from the wear-and-tear of whatever occupying group had been assigned them – without seeming offensively to be doing so. Those who had lived through the experiences of the First World War were more attentive about it than the novices. If those who lived through World War Two had known what their predecessors knew about requisitioning, many would no doubt have taken much more care than they did.

Paintings and artwork were, of course, a first priority. James Pope-Hennessy describes going round Knole with the steward, unhooking Mytenses and Lelys from the wall, and taking Mary Queen of Scots' altar-piece from the chapel. 'He had applied mainly an aesthetic standard to what to "save", and I persuaded him to add some splendid flat and rigid Jacobean men and women to his medley in the vaults.'

Putting paintings in vaults was not always the best solution. There were other hazards besides irresponsible soldiers or German bombs. The Rothschilds' great collection of eighteenth- and nineteenth-century paintings at Waddesdon Manor, removed into the basement when the house was converted into accommodation for evacuee children, was almost destroyed by damp. At Harewood House, which had been an officers' hospital in the First World War and resumed that role in the Second, the paintings were left on the walls but protected by thick sheets of hardboard. Those who could, sent their paintings somewhere else for safekeeping – the Buccleuch Collection, for instance, went to the family homes in Scotland. All contents of great value from Goodwood were also removed and dispersed. The library bookshelves were blocked in with 3-ply; and the main pictures despatched to the West Country as at the time it was thought Hitler's Luftwaffe would never reach there. The Duke of Richmond recounts that the famous Canalettos were first deposited along with many valuable articles of furniture at Messrs. Chapman's Depository at Taunton. 'Our agents for the removal subsequently had nerves about this and moved the Canalettos to the underground cave storehouse of a Mr Lysaght somewhere nearby. At the end of the war Chapman's was burnt down by a spark from a railway engine. Was this some curious figment of the occult?'

Another solution to the storage of artworks was to shut up rooms that contained valuable treasures. This could be done if the house was large enough to fulfil its requisition requirements. For the rest, it was a matter of trying to board up panelling without putting offending nails in the wood; taking down curtains and removing upholstery without tearing them, particularly difficult with old fabrics; removing chandeliers and sconces without breaking them, and so on. In short, the kind of job an experienced museum curator might be able to accomplish but less easy for elderly chatelaines of very large mansions, already suffering the effects of staff shortages. (In some cases the Government came to their aid. The Ministry of Works took it upon itself to protect certain houses with which it was involved, such as Audley End, where even the stair-treads were protected, and Attingham Park, where details such as dados were carefully boarded over.)

For some owners, possession of art treasures exempted them from more onerous duties. Mrs Price Woods of Henley Hall, near Ludlow, told James Lees-Milne, who was visiting in his National Trust capacity, 'If there is any threat of evacuees I shall spread out the art treasures and furniture into more rooms.' Others were less protective about their belongings than they should have been. When the Queen of England found out that the collections in Apsley House had not been removed, she telephoned the Duchess of Wellington and told her that Their Majesties would be over together in person to take them out and store them at Frogmore.

It was not protection of inanimate treasures alone that preoccupied their owners. Lord Rosebery lent Mentmore to his brother-in-law, the Marquess of Crewe, for the duration of the war. He also kept many of his best racehorses there, including Blue Peter, his Derby winner, who was standing at stud. While it was considered quite safe to store works of art at Mentmore, including the Wallace Collection, materials from Westminster Abbey and the Coronation Coach (experts came every few months from London to turn the wheels), there was no such confidence when it came to prize horseflesh. By the end of the war, His Lordship's Derby winner had been sent elsewhere.

A few houses escaped requisitioning or other emergency alterations alto-gether. Evelyn Waugh visited the Sitwells at Renishaw in 1942 and found everything open. 'No evacuees or billeted soldiers; no dust sheets except in the ball room. Banks of potted plants and bowls of roses; piles of new and old books and delicious cooking . . .' (In contrast, Sir George Sitwell's house in Italy, Montegufoni, was requisitioned by the Italian government and used as a repository for paintings from the Uffizi and Pitti Palaces as well as other Tuscan art works.) Petworth was another house that remained inviolate. The Paul Storr plate and the Monteith bowls remained in place, the whole house shuttered and wrapped in dustsheets while Lord Leconfield, plus a housekeeper and a housemaid, sat out the war. (His wife spent it in less happy circumstances, in a mental home.) Houghton Hall in Norfolk was also privately maintained ('just as well,' said the Marquess of Cholmondeley, 'because great damage might have been caused to the many treasures there'). But these were excep-tions. Even a house that was delivered of school, army, hospital or strategic operations, was likely to be threatened by war activities at its boundaries –

trees felled for an airfield, a park dug for a military base, fields fenced off as training grounds.

While all the dismantling was going on, new construction was also often required. Nissen huts sprouted up all over England's parkland, inspiring a young schoolgirl evacuated to Longleat to pen the following lines:

> 'The mystery of a Nissen hut,
> (So elusive, so appealing),
> How much of the thing is sides?
> Or is the whole thing ceiling?'

Emergency accommodations had to be found for evacuees, institutions and local offices. One such structure, promoted with great enthusiasm in the autumn of 1939, was the '*Country Life* Emergency Hut', a modest building looking rather like a toolshed, which the magazine proudly offered to its readers as 'a simple little building that would not be unsightly in any situation, and its particular merit is that after it has served wartime purposes it can be used as a garden house, storeroom, estate office, and so forth.'

It is not only with hindsight that the art of rendering inoperative the big country houses to prepare for war has such profoundly symbolic overtones. James Pope-Hennessy's June 1940 letter to Clarissa Churchill about Knole expresses the elegiac mood already permeating this shadowed world:

'We walked in the great dank gardens in the evening light with wide turf alleys and rhododendron flowers, and urns on pedestals; and the house and the elms; but there was only an illusion of peace and the previous tranquil world, and the whole ordered landscape seemed quivering with imminent destruction.'

Iris Origo strikes the same note when visiting her house in Florence, the Villa Medici, requisitioned by the Germans in 1943. 'When I arrive to sort the furniture the first lorry-full of German soldiers has already arrived, and are installing a telephone in the old chapel. They are perfectly civil and ask for one piece of furniture only: the piano. "One of our officers," they say, "ist ein berühmter Komponist. He has composed an opera about Napoleon!"' . . .

'As I go from one room to another – all now full of German soldiers – I have a strong presentiment that this is the end of something: of this house, of a whole way of living. It will never be the same again.'

Rooms in dustsheets – that seems to be the pre-eminent image of the time. It was as though even the non-requisitioned houses had retired from the fray, de-clawed for the duration. For not only were the interiors stripped and gutted, but the owners themselves were deposed from their little kingdoms, forgoing manors, rents, revenues in virtue of a new, more rigorous regime. A few of those exempt from the war were able to stay at home. Phyllis Furley, a radio decoder at Kedleston during the last months of the war, remembers Viscount Scarsdale in residence, showing young privates round the house. Some, like Lord Bath at Longleat, moved to a wing, if there was a wing. The Buccleuch family moved to a small corner of Drumlanrig Castle, in Dumfriesshire, the rest of it being occupied by St Denis's, a large Edinburgh girls' school. 'As a young sailor on leave from the Royal Navy,' recalls the present Duke of Buccleuch, 'I sometimes used to cause some embarrassment by suddenly appearing in the central courtyard or the Dining Room while the girls were doing gym in their knickers.' Many wives and families with husbands at the war moved to a gatehouse or dower house; still others found refuge in the village with friends, or in other villages with relatives. Where houses had been requisitioned as hospitals, some chatelaines were asked to stay on as commandants.

This wholesale unseating was not always easy, as witness the difficulties endured by Queen Mary, decamped to Badminton. In spite of being accompanied by more than fifty servants and seventy pieces of personal luggage, she was unhappy, restless and homesick, at least in the early years. If this indomitable woman felt that way, how many lesser mortals must have suffered from being wrenched from their homes, seeing their houses and belongings fall into strangers' hands, with no guarantee of restoration. A whole world of country pursuits, elegant house-parties, sporting entertainments and glorious decoration was under wraps, frozen, suspended in time. For some, the life never returned to those rooms. The houses, and all that was in them, were finished. The dustsheets were shrouds.

The First
Occupation

'HOW GRATEFUL ONE WAS at that time for weekends in the country,' wrote John Lehmann about the first year of the war. 'Country houses seemed like islands of the pre-war life.' Then he added, 'Evacuees were, of course, the great problem and endurance test at the beginning: no one likes his house to be invaded suddenly by strangers of unknown habits and unpredictable demands, but the communal emotion, the sense of national duty, fortified hearts against the shock of privacy violated, squalor unmasked and property under siege.'

In the midst of all the other confusion over requisitioning, country houses were islands of security for displaced children in the eyes of the Government, which found itself spending a great deal of effort to get the rest of the country to support it. Public Information Leaflet Number 3, distributed in July 1939, resorted to a subtle form of emotional blackmail in support of its evacuation programme. 'Do not hesitate to register your children under this scheme,' it urged, 'particularly if you live in a crowded area. Of course it means heartache to be separated from your children, but you can be quite sure that they will be well looked after. That will relieve you of one anxiety at any rate. You cannot wish, if it is possible to evacuate them, to let your children experience the dangers and fears of air attack in crowded cities.'

19

Well, no. But parents were being asked to send their school-age children away, to deliver their little ones into the hands of strangers. Hundreds and thousands of them, many of whom had never seen a cow, let alone a stately home, were to be herded into trains with their teachers to some unknown spot in an unknown wilderness known as The Country.

'It would not be possible to let all parents know in advance the place to which each child is to be sent,' continued the leaflet, 'but they would be notified as soon as the movement is over.'

Well, yes. But how many parents can have felt comfortable abandoning their children, along with thousands of others, to an unknown fate, particularly at a time when all lives were under threat of war? 'Work must go on,' declared the leaflet. 'We are not going to win a war by running away. Most of us will have work to do, and work that matters, because we must maintain the nation's life and the production of munitions and other material essential to our war effort . . . Men and women alike will have to stand firm, to maintain our effort for victory.'

The 'evacuable' areas under the government scheme included London and the outlying boroughs in Essex and Middlesex; Portsmouth, Gosport, Southampton, Birmingham, Smethwick, Liverpool, Bootle, Birkenhead, Wallasey, Manchester, Sheffield, Leeds, Bradford, Hull, Newcastle, Gateshead, Edinburgh, Glasgow, Clydebank and Dundee. The names alone have a slightly nightmarish cast; it was the children of these inner-city industrial poor who were being uprooted from their environments in one of the most massive social movements ever contemplated.

The first evacuation took place on 1 September 1939 – approximately 750,000 schoolchildren, along with over 100,000 teachers and helpers. 'It is an exodus bigger than that of Moses,' declared Walter Elliott, Minister of Health. 'It is the movement of ten armies, each of which is as big as the whole Expeditionary Force.' Moses, however, was being followed by a fairly sensible and motivated group of citizens. These city children were going to places they had probably never dreamed of in their little lives. The results were, to say the least, mixed. The first evacuation, during the 'phoney war', was an almost complete flop, with most children returning home by Christmas. But during the Battle of Britain it all happened again, and this time the flock was more accepting of the necessity of the move.

Much has been written about the culture-shock suffered both by the innocent invaders and the equally innocent hosts as the billeting took effect. Stories of head lice, vermin, malnutrition and other horrors circulated like wildfire. 'Woolworth has queues of people buying mackintosh sheeting!' wrote a correspondent from Hampshire to *Time* magazine in October 1939. Sales of Dettol also skyrocketed. 'The war has brought the great unwashed right into the bosoms of the great washed,' as Mollie Panter-Downes put it in *The New Yorker*.

Evelyn Waugh's novel, *Put Out More Flags*, published in 1943, chronicled the progress of a set of frightful children as Basil Seal planted them on one unsuspecting household after another, leaving ruin in their wake. Waugh perfectly presents the tenor of the times when Seal's sister, Barbara Sothill, first meets some evacuees in the village. Mrs Sothill lives, of course, in one of the great country houses, Malfrey, which had been 'built more than two hundred years ago in days of victory and ostentation and lay, spread out, sumptuously at ease, splendid, defenceless and provocative'. After Mrs Sothill generously suggests to a recently-arrived family from Birmingham that they might like to play in the park, one of the mothers exclaims indignantly, 'What's she? Some kind of inspector, I suppose, with her airs and graces. The idea of inviting us into the park. You'd think the place belonged to her the way she goes on.'

In general, local authorities were charged with finding homes for the children, along with hastily-appointed billeting officers, who were mostly the leading gentry of the villages, or harking back to feudal times, the owners of the manor houses. The difficulties were legion. Many houses had already been requisitioned by other organizations, and owners were hard put to find space for extra bodies, however willing in theory to take evacuees in. At one time at Mentmore, for instance, there were over a hundred evacuee children from London in the house, many of them with whooping cough; the artworks from the Wallace Collection; Blue Peter, Lord Rosebery's Derby winner, standing at stud; and Miriam Rothschild, then working at Bletchley, occupying a small suite upstairs. 'So there were a hundred refugees with whooping cough, Blue Peter, the Wallace Collection and me!' Other owners were less than enthusiastic about offering hospitality to the displaced families. 'For the first time I felt like a pariah in the village,' recalls Lady Seebohm of her role attempting to 'place' evacuees from Sheffield in the village of Woodsetts. 'People fled as they saw me walk down the street. Often it was the rougher families who took them in.'

The rougher families, liberated from such problems as the refugee children pissing on the Aubussons or bashing up the Chippendale, also had an eye on the compensations. The government allowance for evacuated children was ten shillings a week for one, and eight shillings and sixpence for each above one. For many working-class parents this was a bigger income than they normally had to support their families: a thought-provoking discovery for many upper-middle-class country folk.

But as has been much commented on since, the most profound discovery was that of the realities of slum life and the effects of poverty on a social group up until then largely unknown. 'We visited a house, a large pleasant dwelling with a good garden near a small village,' wrote an American eyewitness. 'It had been furnished with a minimum of benches, rough tables, wire and camp beds, but had been reduced to a shocking state of filth and untidiness. The rooms, even with the windows open, stank; there were adequate sanitary arrangements, but the children (of whom there were six or seven, from babies to fourteen or so), relieved themselves everywhere but the place provided for the purpose; in a word, a decent house had become a squalid slum in a week.'

Stories of the horrors were not confined to England. Iris Origo, writing her diary in Italy in 1943 about her own young refugees, said, 'We have had, of course, to struggle with their hair (most of them have had their heads shaved), but otherwise their "habits" contrast most favourably with what I have heard of the little evacuees in English villages.'

A school headmaster evacuated to the west of England reported that in many cases the billeting officers refused to billet children on their friends, so the smaller cottages were forced to accept them. In some cases, the cottages belonged to the billeting officers, through the tied system of feudally-structured estates. How could you say no to your landlord? 'In cases where children are in large houses, they are usually left entirely to the maids, who thus get the extra work.'

Certainly the three evacuees who came to live with Princess Alice, Duchess of Gloucester, at Barnwell Manor, stayed in the staff quarters and were looked after by the cook and the Duchess's secretary. However, the redoubtable Princess Alice saw to the exercise of the three evacuees herself by playing cricket with them out on the lawn, and she read to them before they were tucked in at night. 'One morning they got up at four o'clock with the intention of walking back to London; but luckily went in the wrong direction and soon got tired. When reprimanded they said the country was so dull and they wanted to see more of the raids and bombs.'

While some houses still had maids to look after the evacuee children, others, less fortunate with staff, took the ingenious step of conscripting the children into service instead. What could be more thoughtful of the lady of the manor than to take the step of training small visitors to dust, clean, wash dishes, and even polish the shoes? For the shrewd operator, wartime can thus transform adversity into advantage.

Whoever did the housework, many chatelaines had to cope with the problem of feeding ten or more little mouths, and columns such as Penelope Chetwode's in *Country Life* were designed to help one cope. 'If you live in the country and have evacuees billeted on you,' she wrote briskly in September 1939, 'rabbit should be included at least once in the weekly menu.' The author then included several rabbit menus, including Boiled Rabbit with Onion Sauce, Lapin au Cari, and Lapin en Casserole. She added this warning: 'The first rule about rabbit is, don't ask the people who are going to eat it whether they like it or not. So many people have an idiotic idea that the very thought makes them sick, either because they have never had it properly cooked or because they are well-read in Beatrix Potter and can't bear to think of devouring the Flopsy Bunnies ...' (It is doubtful whether many of the evacuees had ever heard of Beatrix Potter. More probably, their objections to rabbit were on culinary grounds. Most of them firmly believed in a permanent diet of fish and chips, plus a 'beano' on Sunday, which, according to one London boy, meant celebrating Dad's Saturday paycheck with a Sunday breakfast of bananas and beer.)

One of the many difficulties was finding space for schooling for the evacuee children. The public boarding schools, in most cases, had already made arrangements. Blenheim Palace took in the boys from Malvern, Lancing College in Sussex welcomed Westminster, and St Paul's boys found a home on the estate of Lord Downshire in Wokingham. Other school-age children were deposited in unlikely places like Lacock Abbey, where they had their lessons in the South Gallery and used the crypt as a cloakroom, or Odam Hill Children's Farm, a remote home school in North Devon, which must have taken a little adjusting to. There were cows and horses everywhere, who frightened the small children unaccustomed to country flora and fauna. The hens pecked at the children's fingers, and the goats were hardly more friendly. Not very reassuring replacements for one's desperately-missed parents, or the security of home, be it ever so humble.

In June 1940, at the height of the evacuations, the Morale Emergency Committee reported to the Policy Committee of the Home Office that 'class feeling was a major threat to public calm'. In June 1941 another report called the attention of the Home Planning Committee 'to the widespread irritation caused in country districts that evacuees were not billeted in the larger homes'.

The problem was not only the feeling that some of the privileged classes were escaping their wartime responsibilities, but that these people were also continuing to have a jolly good time at home while everyone else was suffering, as this disingenuous little item in *Queen* magazine in October 1939 shows:

'In the country, hostesses who have not handed over their houses for hospitals or some kind of Government centre are in many cases entertaining their own London friends there indefinitely.' The magazine then hastily adds that 'Lady Brickan-Jardine at Birfield Park [Bracknell, Berks.] has not only friends with her but a party of eighteen evacuated boys with their teachers!'

The spirit, of course, was willing. 'I want them to see the spring spreading through the countryside,' declared Mr Kenneth Lindsay, Parliamentary Secretary to the Board of Education about their plan to 'scatter' London and city schoolchildren like wildflowers over the fields of England. But Mr Lindsay's charming notion was perhaps more accurately expressed in this note from an urban district councillor for Buckinghamshire. On noting that 17,000 children had been evacuated from London into the county, swelling the population of Bletchley by twenty-five per cent, he remarked, 'Of the few who returned no one on earth would have billeted, and they did the wisest thing eventually to return to the hovels from whence they came.' The Chief Billeting Officer from Hitchin Rural District Council no doubt reflected the feeling of a great many country people when he said, 'I'm afraid that however undesirable these people may be we cannot and must not, for the present, send them back to London.'

The Blitz evacuations had little of the organization of the earlier groups, lacking, no doubt, a homegrown Moses. Having been bombed out of their homes, hundreds of London families were simply told to leave the area, with no other alternative arrangements being made for them. In Diana Brinton-Lee's diaries, she describes seeing some Green Line buses, full of dispossessed people, mostly women and children, without money or a change of clothes, driving aimlessly from one centre to another for as long as five days in a futile effort to get help.

For these sad cases, perhaps the point made by Commander A. V. S. Yates, in a letter to an American friend, rings true:

'The tremendous social experiment of shifting the town population to the country has revealed, as far anyhow as the mothers and children are concerned, that country people – living in many cases round the Manors as in the old feudal days – are, though much poorer in worldly monetary wealth, infinitely richer in standards of cleanliness, happiness, kindliness, comfort and contentment than the townsfolk.'

It was not only children who were placed in 'safe' country houses. One was expected to open one's house for almost anyone, military or civilian. The Emergency Powers (Defence) Act of 1939 laid down that the cost was tenpence per night for one soldier, and eightpence for each additional one. Breakfast was eightpence; dinner elevenpence; tea threepence and supper fivepence. But these individual rules were rapidly overtaken as whole houses were drafted by the Military and the other fighting forces. Paying guests were another breed of evacuee, such as officers' wives with Nanny and three children, 'willing to pay very small weekly sum for large, sunny rooms with piano, central heating and use of bathroom', or middle-aged couples, 'willing to help with the housework'. These situations often became as critical as that of the city children, since gentility required an even greater show of sharing and caring.

But it was the city children who aroused the most controversy and revealed the underlying cracks in a society unused to this kind of enforced occupation. 'Country people are willing to do all they can to help,' wrote the Reverend T. C. Cuningham of Shrewsbury to *The Times* in September 1939, 'but their mode of living is so different to that of the town dweller that I cannot see that the present method of billeting will ever be a success.'

There were, to be sure, some successes. A few evacuees learned to love the countryside, and stayed. Some returned home but stayed in contact with their rural hosts. But whatever the truth of the evacuations, there is no doubt that it was an instant education in class consciousness. The exposure of country house-owners to the sickness, uncleanliness and lack of civilization of these inner-city children was both horrifying and genuinely shocking to them. The evacuated parents' and children's boredom, loneliness, isolation and fear, at being pitchforked into an unfamiliar and mostly unwelcoming world, accumulated into a stockpile of anger and resentment that was to be extensively drawn on in the political upheavals after the war.

Blackout Country

As soon as war was declared in September 1939, one prescient mother raced seventy-five miles to spend a night with her son while she could still get petrol. She was old enough to know only too well what lay ahead. Even then, the roads were already clogged with troops, lorries, vans, tanks and fatigue parties – the rush-hour traffic of wartime.

As well as attempting to protect family treasures from the hazards of requisitioning, and coping with influxes of alien children, country house-owners were also confronted with one of the most tedious and exacting duties provoked by the war – the blackout. All through the summer of 1939 signs of the grim days to come had flooded people's consciousness. Civil Defence leaflets were hastily printed and distributed across the country, giving instructions about the wearing of gas masks, explanations of the evacuations, and instructions for the blackout, perhaps the single most trying condition civilians were to endure. 'On the outbreak of hostilities, all external lights and street lighting would be totally extinguished so as to give hostile aircraft no indication as to their whereabouts,' explained the Civil Defence brochure cheerfully. 'The motto for safety will be "Keep it dark!" '

The idea of covering every window was difficult enough for a small house or flat, but a task of almost insuperable magnitude for the larger stately homes. Some country houses were lucky enough to have shutters, but many had leaded, mullion, Georgian, or Gothic windows, framed by ancient curtains entirely unsuited to the challenge of total blackness. People rummaged through attics and trunks for old scraps of stuff to hang up, and were often forced to purchase suitable material for the purpose, allowing manufacturers of Bolton Twill or Lancaster Blind Cloth an unexpected bonanza. In fact, stocks quickly ran out and sheets, blankets and tablecloths were brought out of linen cupboards and requisitioned for duty, hastily dyed to a suitable dark shade to comply with the regulations. Sanderson's, the decorating firm, cleverly came up with the idea of double-sided wallpaper, one side black, to be pasted on the glass of your windows, and the other side a pretty chintz or pastel colour, thus brightening the interior of your rooms. (A six-yard roll of this ingenious problem-solver cost two shillings.)

People with every kind of skill were brought in to help with the emergency. One of the evacuees at Dunton Hall, on the south coast, turned out to be a useful carpenter. He made some light window frames to fit the windows. With dark material tacked on them they formed a perfect blackout, allowing not a chink of light to escape. Less fortunate was a Hampshire correspondent, whose house had sixty-two windows and skylights. 'I was determined "Adolf" was not going to put me to great expense, so wonderful and fearful are our contraptions, and it takes half an hour every night to shut up the house.' She also enjoyed the visit of the Police Sergeant who came to inspect her windows. 'He fell down the conservatory step headlong into the plants, tin helmet and gas masks and all and I had to pull him out ...'

Hard on the heels of this tiresome and depressing government requirement came another. Petrol rationing, introduced in September 1939, was the first blow to civilization as every country-dweller knew it. From that date, you were allowed 200 miles, per month, per car. (All kinds of travel from then on was discouraged. On trains, passengers were confronted with notices demanding, 'Is your journey really necessary?') To city people, with public transport at least an alternative, the petrol limitation was tolerable. The restriction was one of the most formidable challenges of the war, on the other hand, to country-dwellers, for whom a car was almost more essential than the telephone. Those living in the more remote outposts of rural England were entirely dependent on the old family jalopy to take the children to school, shop for groceries or transport animals and people to their various daily destinations. Elizabeth Longford was at Water Eaton, outside Oxford, when rationing was introduced. 'We had to draw up a rota for shopping. With about twenty people living in the house, it was quite an undertaking. A school rota also had to be organized, since two children and a governess needed fetching to and from Oxford every weekday.'

Cycle shops did a roaring trade. Pony traps were dusted off. The issues raised by petrol rationing were enthusiastically taken up by old soldiers and other experts, who devised all sorts of ingenious solutions to the problem:

'Since rationing of petrol came in I have managed to get about 18 m.p.g. out of my Lincoln Zephyr by the following method of driving,' wrote Captain C. J. Orde to the readers of *Country Life* in October 1939. 'As little choking as possible; never using the great power of acceleration; never exceeding 20 m.p.h. and coasting whenever possible ... This is of course,' he adds, 'not very exciting.'

The good captain's recommendations may have saved petrol, but some people complained that the resulting snail's pace caused as much menace on the roads as those racing along at 60 mph trying to get home before the blackout. The combination of petrol rationing with the blackout became positively lethal. For if you drove at night you were only allowed to use dimmed or side lights, and the task of negotiating winding country lanes on low beam was hardly conducive to a relaxed journey home. Various manufacturers took advantage of the situation and started producing headlight covers and luminous bumper strips. Fashionable stores such as Harrods suggested chic ways for pedestrians to avoid danger at night, such as white hats and armlets, luminous decorations, and other see-in-the-dark accessories. But the number of adult pedestrians killed on the roads in England and Wales tripled between August and September 1939 – from 168 in August to 550 in September. This was largely due to the blackout.

Not only were the roads almost impenetrable once the sun had set, there was also the danger of failure to see animals wandering about, a concern that, needless to say, aroused the anxiety of the English even more than their own personal safety. Suggestions flew about the country as to how the animals might be protected. One such idea was that the New Forest ponies (a particular problem, since they often roamed free) should be painted with white stripes so that cars could see them in the dark. The almost surreal quality of country life under petrol rationing led Major Jarvis, columnist for *Country Life*, to conclude: 'Those of our friends who live over 20 miles away will now belong to the same category as others of our acquaintance who live in India and the Far East, and who receive a card from us every Christmas.'

The hair-raising requirement of driving at night without lights, as part of the universal blackout after dark, was exacerbated by a further complication that occurred in 1940, when the German invasion was expected at any minute. To confuse the enemy, signposts, railway station names and all other identifying place names were blocked out, turned the wrong way, or simply removed. The results of this were interesting, to say the least. Even to the experienced rural traveller, it is not always fun finding one's way at night to a house deep in the remotest countryside, negotiating murky hedge-lined lanes and winding driveways, however good one's host's instructions may be. With misleading or vanished signposts, plus minimal lights, the novice might well find the challenge insurmountable – quite apart from the fact that suspicion of strangers abounded at this time of invasion fever. A correspondent describes with wry amusement the experience of a government official in Northampton, driving in a hired car via a short cut through some country roads. 'A few miles out of town the old bean got properly lost so he stopped to enquire the way but everyone was a stranger to the place, or didn't know, until at last he saw an RAC man. He apologized for belonging to the AA, and explained his difficulty; the man listened and then said, "You have a Northampton registration on your car, and if you don't know your own country it's damn well time you did." Then he got on his bike and rode off. The official bean was a Londoner and never knew where the car had been registered!'

There were ancillary rules given to car owners during the alarmist period when the Hun was supposedly at the gate. If you left your car unattended, you had to make sure you locked it, for fear, supposedly, that an invading German might hop into it and drive off. This was not a requirement that sat lightly with country folk, who were not at all accustomed to locking their cars. One county lady left her Airedale in her car, but failed to lock the vehicle. When questioned by the police, she assured them that neither 20 nor 200 invaders would have been suffered to lay a finger on the car with her beloved pet inside. The constabulary was not amused.

Rationing was not limited to petrol, of course. Electricity could be used up to two-thirds of normal capacity, which meant somewhat feeble central heating for those houses blessed with such a luxury. (The winter of 1939 was a notoriously cold one.) But of greater interest to almost everyone was the question of food rationing. The worst deprivations were sugar and fresh fruits, much of which came from overseas. Rations were generally apportioned as follows, for two people, per week: two ounces of butter, four ounces of margarine, one ounce of lard, three ounces of bacon, two ounces of cheese, eight ounces of sugar, and two eggs.

Cooking became an imaginative exercise, particularly for those not used to it. Nancy Mitford told her sister, Jessica (whom she called Susan), a tragic tale

29

of egg-rationing. 'I was staying with Farve at the Mews. He'd been awfully ill, but one day he roused himself and said, "I think I should fancy a boiled egg, Koko." Mabel was doing for us but she had gone out, so I boiled up the water and threw the egg in. Susan, the most sinister white stuff started coming out of it, like an octopus, so I threw it away. Then I did another one, and the same thing happened. Then the third one, same thing. Oh dear I was sad, there went our whole week's egg ration, one each for Farve, Mabel and me.'

The limitations on eggs and bacon, plus the loss of citrus fruits such as grapefruits and oranges, the staples of any right-thinking man's breakfast, were a bitter blow. Even Princess Alice, Duchess of Gloucester, was not immune. A South African doctor sent her a case of oranges but Lord Woolton, Minister of Food, would not allow her to accept them. 'Harry [the Duke] was furious.'

Thanks to rationing, farmers were suddenly the most courted members of country society. Although the Government attempted to prevent a kind of 'grey market' developing (one grocer was fined thirty pounds for selling butter without a ration card), most people managed to achieve the odd fresh egg or butter from the local dairies. Inspectors came round checking who was growing what, causing any amount of confusion, witness this report from a Miss Jenny Prosser:

'And what does the Government say now? "Produce eggs," and in the next breath, "oh, you can't have any corn for feeding fowls." And then along comes a fellow in a fine car with a chauffeur and says, "Now, Miss Prosser, you've got too much ground for those fowls, you must put down potatoes." "But the fowls must run," says I. "But not too far," says he. I looks at him again hard, and believe me, it was the same fellow who had got Farmer Smith over Barnton fined five pounds two years come September for putting down too many spuds – and then got him fined again for selling the big ones!'

With a little wheeling and dealing on the side, many country families found ways of enjoying a few luxuries from time to time. Vita Sackville-West sent butter from the farm at Sissinghurst to Virginia Woolf, who broke off a lump and ate it neat. Anthony Powell tells the story of a visit to the Sitwells at Renishaw and sending off his wife, Violet, with Edith Sitwell, to the fish-monger's in Sheffield, in pursuit of fresh salmon. Violet had informed Edith of the best ways to cook the fish, ending with the words: 'Then you make the tail into kedgeree.' Edith swept into the shop and asked the fishmonger if he had a salmon, explaining that they wanted it for making kedgeree.

'The fishmonger went pale. Had the days of the Bourbons returned? Lucullus himself might have thought twice before devoting a whole newly caught salmon to kedgeree; anyway while Rome was at war.' The salmon, however, was produced. It was then left behind by mistake in another shop. 'But all was well in the end,' relates Mr Powell, 'the salmon being put on a train just in time to reach Renishaw for dinner.' This kind of performance, one may assume, could only have been pulled off in wartime by (and for) people such as the Sitwells.

André Simon, writing in *The Field* in 1940, urges his readers to resort to wine. 'With the Riviera out of reach for most of us and Florida out of bounds to all of us there is a grave danger of letting depression sneak in and make our lives miserable. We must not let it . . . We must not be depressed. We must drink wine, the joy that is wine, the good wine that maketh glad the heart of man.'

While those who had the joy that is wine in their cellars (probably safely tucked away with the family paintings and other heirlooms) could tipple away merrily, the deprived classes were left with beer, which was very soon in very short supply, if indeed it could be obtained at all. Pubs began opening at irregular times, and the complaint was that the troops could rush into the village at all hours and drain the pubs dry before the locals had time to leave work, get to the pub and sink a drop down their own throats. The Irish, many of whom were employed to help build airfields and other military installations at the beginning of the war, found ways round this problem, needless to say. The Irishmen who were helping to put up Polebrooke airfield, near Peterborough, for instance, used to get blind drunk every night. How could they do it on the meagre liquor supplies at the village pub? It was revealed that they were bubbling coal gas into milk, apparently a well-known intoxicant. The milk takes off the toxins so instead of killing them it simply made them drunk. It is unlikely the Irish were allowed to keep this secret to themselves for long.

The food shortage introduced new rules of etiquette for weekend visits to country houses, as Mollie Panter-Downes explained. 'Rationing has made it perfectly in order for the weekend guest to arrive with his own little parcel of butter, which he places in the hand of the butler who takes his suitcase. If the guest wants to express lyrical appreciation of the visit, his hostess would much rather he said it not with orchids but with something like a pound of Demerara sugar or a few petrol coupons.' Petrol coupons were supposed to be non-transferable, but as with so much of country house life during the war, the rules were always bendable if you knew the right people, the right garages, and the right parts of the country.

The desperation for fresh fruit and vegetables became acute as the war went into its second year. One gentleman was driving home too fast and crashed the car in a country lane. Some RAF men helped him out. Looking dazed, he tried to remember something he had in the car that was evidently very important to him. 'Two cauliflowers,' he finally mumbled. 'I bought them in Wareham and they cost eighteenpence each. I was hurrying home with them.'

The food crisis created some hallucinatory situations. Sparrows, starlings, rooks, swans and seagulls were seen for sale in Smithfield Meat Market. And Nancy Mitford told 'Susan' an even stranger bird story. Some friends of Nancy's had been given a goose, a treasured treat in days when meat or fowl were virtually unobtainable. 'They wrung its neck and plucked it, and put it in the fridge meaning to cook it the next day,' Nancy related. 'Susan, in the morning they took it out and IT WAS STILL ALIVE, giving them the most baleful look. So they rushed down to the village and used their last clothing coupon to buy some tweed to make it a coat. It stalked around in that coat looking ABSOLUTELY LIVID, for the whole rest of the war.'

An unexpected new shortage emerged in the autumn of 1940. NO ONIONS. It turned out that England depended almost entirely for its onions on Italy, Spain, Egypt, North Africa and the Netherlands, none of which, needless to say, was at that time doing much exporting of the valued vegetable. Why England could not grow its own was not clear; much hand labour was required, and apparently onions did not ripen well in the English climate. Very soon everyone was crying for onions. The prize raffle at a charity event was no longer a car, or a bottle of wine, but a pound of onions. There was a scheme to start onion clubs, whereby collections would be sent to the men in the Forces, who were similarly deprived. A synthetic flavouring was produced called 'ex-onion', which pleased nobody. The solution was to grow your own onions (it turned out to be not so difficult, after all), and a year later the crisis passed.

One onion story lingers, however. The place is Sissinghurst, in 1942, where a Brigadier, plus five officers, cook and batman, are to be billeted for the night. 'It was at that moment,' Harold Nicolson wrote to his sons, 'that Mummy remembered the onions stored on the floor of the loft. They number between two and three thousand. She said that the Army always stole onions and that we must remove them at any cost before they arrived. I said that we were only having a Brigadier and his officers, and that a) they would probably not want to steal more than three onions each, and b) we should not miss them much if they did. She said that you could never tell with officers nowadays, so many of them were promoted from the ranks. So we got three sacks and two shovels and all afternoon, till darkness came, we carried the sacks across to the Priest's

House and spread them on the floor of Pat's room. We had scarcely finished with the last onion when the Brigadier appeared. He was a nice well-behaved man and looked so little like an onion-stealer that Mummy at once asked him to dinner.'

In order to overcome the long-term problem of food, the Government instituted a vast ploughing-up programme. Roughly thirty per cent of the country's energy requirements came from the land. During the 1914–18 war, that percentage was brought up to forty-two per cent. For the new war, it was hoped to reach fifty per cent. This meant reclaiming millions of acres for arable use. In 1916, there were eleven million acres of arable land in England and Wales, rising to twelve and a half million in 1918. By 1938 that figure had shrunk back again to nine million acres, the rest reverting to grassland. Yet during that time the population rose by more than five million. The war brought these grim statistics out into the open for the first time, revealing a waste of indigenous resources that was not lost on the Government or the farming community.

The ploughing-up campaign changed the face of the countryside almost more than any other single factor during World War Two, except for the German bombs. The Minister of Agriculture, Sir Reginald Dorman-Smith, stated in the autumn of 1939 that the goal was to reclaim two million acres within the year – by June 1940. Farmers were asked to plough up ten per cent of their present grassland, and sow wheat, potatoes, oats, barley, beans, peas, rye or mixed corn. 'The furrow is our trench,' was the theme of the campaign, paraphrased from a remark by Winston Churchill. A subsidy of two pounds an acre was offered to the farmers, provided the grassland had been down for seven years or more, or was in worthless scrub condition. The carrot was hardly adequate, but it worked. County after county reported its turnover: Gloucestershire – 35,000 acres, Suffolk – 26,000 acres, Wiltshire – 40,000 acres, and so on. Improved equipment speeded up the process. By June 1940, the astonishing figure was achieved – over two million acres had been brought back to arable land. In its modest way, this achievement was as significant a contribution to the war effort as any of the military campaigns.

While many country people were eager to help, turning parkland into hayfields, and herbaceous borders into vegetable patches, not all hor-ticulturalists were equally enthusiastic. In the last war, it was said, many beautiful gardens had been destroyed by overzealous food growers. Let not this happen again, pleaded garden lovers. To institutionalize the issue, the County War Agricultural Committees issued instructions that half a garden might be preserved for flowers, the rest being made over to vegetables or foodstuffs.

While the ploughing-up scheme did wonders for partridges, bringing them back in large numbers to the fields (along with guns), its benefit to fox-hunting was less apparent. Hunting went on, of course, though with depleted packs and staff, most of those on horseback being under fifteen or over fifty. It was the over-fifties who encouraged the continuation of the sport, recalling how much solace hunting had provided homecoming members of the Forces during the Great War. 'We kept it going then, and we hope to do so now,' was the feeling. What exercised supporters more than the size of the hunt was the increasing laxness over dress, which caused one irate hunting type to resort to pen and paper. 'The opening meets have come and gone,' he wrote in November 1939, 'and I am frankly surprised to see how many people still turn out in tweed jackets and bowlers, instead of correct hunting dress, however simple. It is as though the line taken is that all formality may go by the board because, forsooth, we are at war!'

The encouragement to hunt was limited to a few country enthusiasts, since, forsooth, most active members were absent. Nor was there much incentive from Whitehall, unlike during the First War, when the cavalry still existed, and the War Office had a vested interest in the breeding of horses and the continuation of hunting. A few horses (mostly hunters) were commandeered for action, but nothing like the numbers used in 1914, and hounds no longer went on active service, as they had in the Peninsular War, when packs of hounds were part and parcel of the Duke of Wellington's headquarters staff.

While animals might no longer play a major role in the hostilities, nothing preoccupied people in the country more than their fate at home. Would the children's ponies stampede during an air raid? Would darling Fluffy have a nervous breakdown? Probably not; but there was a report that in one garden, which housed an aviary, all the birds were found dead after a bombing raid – of terror, it was thought. The Duchess of Gloucester observed that her polo ponies proved particularly susceptible to the vibration of aircraft engines. 'If one of our planes passed overhead they paid no attention, but when a German one did they began to tremble and get fidgety. German engines made a different sound – anumb, anumb, anumb – and the ponies recognized this and associated it with danger. It was the same with the bull mastiff we had; he was terrified of German planes, wriggling under the bed or sofa as soon as he heard them coming.'

All sorts of pet protection were proposed, including gas-proof kennels with sound-proof walls. Recommendations for your dog's Wartime Dinner filled the food columns, with menus such as offal, old cows', horses' or bullocks' blood, and sheep's or pigs' trotters. *The Times* carried advertisements offering sanctuary to evacuating dogs from 7/6d a week. People pleaded that the dachshund should not be reviled for its German origins (another hangover from the last war). But perhaps the most frightening experience for a dog was not, in the end, the bombs or the air raids, but the alarming peculiarities suddenly displayed by one's mistress. Take the case, for instance, of the lady owner of a terrier, who put on her gas mask without warning, and then bent down to play with her pet. The dog took one look, ran out, and was never seen again.

Holding the Fort

THE MEN HAD GONE. At least, most able-bodied men had gone, in uniform, to do or die. This left children, old men – many of whom remembered the last war and threw themselves with enthusiasm into whatever service was available to them – and women, old, young, brave, cowardly, efficient, inexperienced, merry and desperate, thousands of women thrust for the first time into the forefront of their own and their family's lives.

As in the First World War, there were conscientious objectors, like Ralph and Frances Partridge, who stayed at Ham Spray House in Wiltshire, and took in refugees of various kinds for the duration of the war. There was also another small upper-class group of people opposed to the war. These were supporters of Hitler. A thread of attachment came down, of course, from the Royal Family itself, whose German origins once again, as in 1914, caused some embarrassment. Members of the Mitford family were probably the most well-known pro-Nazis at the time. Most of the others kept their loyalties to themselves (although Lady Binning disclosed her anti-democratic, pro-German allegiances over tea to James Lees-Milne in 1944), and it is not a subject happily raised in Britain today, particularly in view of the spate of material now being released about collaboration in France. Henry Fairlie was reflecting this unease when he recently wrote, 'What was unnerving in Britain was to wonder who would have collaborated if Hitler had invaded and occupied the Island, not only among the titled, the successful, and the powerful, but among one's own friends and acquaintances.'

But for the rest, most of those living in the country became involved almost at once in some form of war work. It might be manning an ambulance station in the local village, looking after evacuees, organizing relief work for the wounded, running a mobile YMCA canteen, and so on. Memberships of volunteer organizations swelled to overflowing. 'Morris 10s, their windscreens plastered with notices that they are engaged on business of the ARP or WVS ... rock down quiet country lanes propelled by firm-lipped spinsters who yesterday could hardly have said "boo" to an aster,' wrote Mollie Panter-Downes.

The war was no respecter of persons, and women from every stratum of society were expected to man (so to speak) the barricades. Duchesses and dairymaids alike were required to make their contributions to the war effort. Never was the sense of *noblesse oblige* more rewarding than at this time, exercised here possibly in its last legitimate incarnation. The two journals of the upper classes, *Tatler* and *Queen,* rivalled each other in chronicling the progress of the war in the bastions of privilege, as our brave hostesses welcomed schools, hospitals and other war-torn groups into their beautiful country houses or carried on local duties as though nothing untoward was happening to their grand old world.

We read of Mrs Joshua Fielden, of Kineton House, in Warwickshire, for instance, Vice-President of the Red Cross, Chairman of the local Women's Land Army, and organizer of the Warwickshire War Supplies Service, who instituted a local salvage collection and a working party for making bandages. 'There are also twelve evacuees happily installed in some of the rooms over the stables who are having the time of their young lives.' A typical item was this one about the Dowager Countess of Airlie, who had taken charge of the Red Cross activities in her county of Angus while the Duchess of Montrose was looking after the work in Arran. 'Lady Airlie has fifty-five work parties including the one in the castle, and she and her helpers are naturally proud of the fact that in a few days they were able to equip a local hospital of 60 beds with all the dressings and garments that it needed ...'

In houses all over Britain, similar activities were taking place. The names read like a page from *Debrett's*: Lady Zia Wernher as Commandant of a Red Cross hospital, Lady Ashley driving a mobile canteen, Violet, Countess of Leconfield (shortly before she was institutionalized) in a tin hat riding a motorbike round the grounds, the Hon. Lady Longman surrounded by evacuated schoolchildren. Hundreds of them plunged into action in the old feudal way, opening up their houses or going out into the countryside dispensing bandages and good cheer.

With or without a title, every kind of expertise was required. Author Dorothy Black took a Mechanised Transport Training course, to be able to drive wounded in ambulances or other duties required when things began to hum. 'Looking like a decayed railway guard, in that kind of hat, a tubular khaki skirt, stout shoes and thick stockings ... We have things on our tunics too, like blue paste forget-me-nots.'

The most serious problem facing these women was the lack of manpower. Always there had been men on the estate or in the village to fix the boiler, polish the tackle, dig the flowerbed, plough the fields, do all the heavy jobs considered unsuitable for the weaker sex. Suddenly there was no one to do this work – except other women. A few agricultural workers on large estates were exempt from war service, and men over military age were willing but not always able to contribute the requisite muscle. The Women's Land Army, under its director, Lady Gertrude Denman, came to the rescue. Former milliners, tap-dancers, secretaries, girls leaving home for the first time were made to drive tractors, clean stables, milk cows, harvest beets and sow potatoes. By the end of 1939, 30,000 women had volunteered for the Women's Land Army at a wage of 28 shillings a week. By 1943 the number had risen to 56,000.

Some recruits found it difficult to adjust to rural life, for it was literally hard labour, and many of the women had left homes and families for unknown and often isolated destinations. But others discovered pleasure in the experience. Here is one young gardener who went to work for a titled lady near Salisbury:

'On Monday we are to be photographed for the press and they want us to be setting out onion plants for the new bed. We call it "the onion bed" but Lady L. says it is to be known as "the old rose garden" to show what she has sacrificed, I suppose. Great amusement today as the butler turned out in a brand new boiler suit and cap and is to learn to work the water pump from the engineer. He is usually dressed à la butler and very pompous. We understand it is to avoid military service and be called an engineer and essential to the water plant.' The young apprentice loved her work, which she took on instead of teaching. 'This is much nicer, so far. The war has brought me here. Some good things come out of the evilest.'

The other crisis was less susceptible to a solution, and had a much more profound effect on the social fabric of the country. Until the war, a full complement of butlers, maids and other below-stairs personnel was par for the course in most large country houses in England. At a stroke, this domestic army disappeared, and many of them never returned. The war had in effect made domestic service obsolete for most working-class women, who discovered they could find good jobs with better pay elsewhere. The loss in many cases was critical. Chatelaines of rattlingly empty and dust-gathering houses sent out desperate calls for help, not only to a domestic class which had so suddenly evaporated, but to anyone, including the elderly or people who under normal circumstances would have been insulted by the appeal.

'Titled lady offers unfurnished five-roomed cottage in Cambridgeshire village to two persons over military or registration age, one for garden, one for work in owner's house . . .'

'A comfortable home in country near Bath is offered to mother and child under four by lady and gentleman with small daughter in return for light domestic duties. No remuneration is offered or expected. Only gentlewoman who understands the country and is prepared to appreciate a very reasonable proposition need apply . . .'

The shortage resulted in people being obliged to hire totally unsuitable or untrained help, a problem that seems to have aroused tempers even more than the German bombs. 'No one denies that there are shining examples of efficient and willing domestic workers,' wrote E. M. Delafield in *Country Life* in 1941. 'But there are a very much greater number of unwilling, inefficient, selfish and over-paid ones.' Discussion raged as to how to raise the status of housemaids.

Rosina Harrison, Lady Astor's personal maid, described the war period as a time of 'enlightenment' for the employer class. In her memoir, *Rose: My Life in Service,* she writes, 'In many places where for years scant attention had been paid to kitchens and the servants' quarters below stairs, mistresses were now paying the penalty. They were having to work down there themselves and, with the bombing, suddenly the basement rooms became the most important in the house – and the most lived in. Yet many of them were damp, dark, poorly heated and their cooking and cleaning facilities were old-fashioned.'

But perhaps the most dramatic example of the domestic crisis came as the result of an unusual gamble played by an American lady, who advertised for a girl to do general housework, promised a good home for the right person, and kept for the end this munificent inducement: 'Can wear my mink coat on day off.' Little did she know what demon she had unleashed. Within 24 hours 600 young women had applied for the position, asking whether it was really true about the mink coat. The irony would not have been lost on Genet: the mistress and the maid changing clothes and changing roles, the traditional relationship unravelling under the weight and power invested in a fur coat.

Rosina Harrison was one of the Old School who, born and bred to service, was devoted to Lady Astor and the Astor family. She found something to treasure in the changing relationship between master and servant. 'We were family. We'd soldiered together, looked death in the face and suffered the loss of many friends. We'd been shown qualities which no other circumstances would have demonstrated to us, and had shared emotions that would otherwise have remained hidden. We'd liked what we'd seen and these things were now ties as strong as those of class and birth. They are bonds that few if any will ever know again.'

The exceptional demands made upon those who stayed at home affected society from top to bottom. Women who had never had to do anything for themselves suddenly discovered astonishing capabilities and reserves of energy. Take Mrs R. S. Hudson, wife of the Minister of Agriculture, who started a landgirls' hostel on her husband's farm in Pewsey Vale, Wiltshire. Without using a single coupon, and with only five pounds' worth of furniture, she transformed an empty stable building into a residential club for twenty landgirls. She helped to start a British War Relief home in Kent for women factory workers. Meanwhile, she also continued to run her own farm in Oxfordshire of 330 acres, 150 sheep and 53 pedigree Ayrshire cattle. Multiple responsibilities developed as the war progressed. Mrs Cantrell Hubbersty turned her home, Ragdale Hall in Leicestershire, into the county equipment store for all Red Cross convalescent homes. In addition, she ran a Red Cross clothing centre, and also worked for relatives of the wounded and prisoners abroad. Lady Danesbury of Waltham House, Melton Mowbray, managed 675 acres of land, raised cattle in stockyards, was responsible for all the Belvoir Hunt horses, and three nights a week from 8 pm to 6 am was on duty at the Melton Mowbray ARP Depot.

Wives also found themselves assuming their husbands' official duties in the country, such as in the hunting field. Lady Ashton took the place of her husband as MFH of the Heythrop, Mrs Heber Percy, the Cotswold, Mrs Frances Pitt, the Wheatland, Mrs Arkwright, the North Warwickshire, and so on. Needless to say, there was some opposition to this distressing break with tradition among a few die-hards marinating in memories of old wars and old rituals. Can women really run a hunt? they asked doubtfully. Lady grooms and whippers-in do not have voices suitable for rating hounds, and will surely have less control over unruly members . . . Putting women in the garden also raised questions. Can she perform the heavy tasks? Will she tackle the compost heap? (Vita Sackville-West would have scoffed with the rest of her sex.)

The less well-off were equally motivated by the stringencies of war. Struggling with food rationing, saving scraps, planting vegetables, re-styling clothes or swapping them, women revealed a resilience and an inventiveness that probably would have surprised even them, if they had had time to think about it. Women who had always taken the subsidiary role were now becoming leaders, such as Nella Last, a young mother who kept a wartime diary, and who complained to it in 1943, 'I run my house like a business: I have had to, to get all done properly, everything fitted in. Why, then, should women not be looked on as partners, as "business women"?'

Emergencies created by the war turned women into political animals. Take the Great Jam Scandal. Instructions were always being despatched from the Government to conserve food, and in the summer of 1941, shortly before fruit-harvest time, a directive was issued that housewives were not to be allowed to make their own jam, but must sell their fruits and berries to professional jam-makers who would do the preserving and bottling for them. The idea! The insult! Inspired by a group of militant jam-makers in Westmorland, women all over the country revolted. The Women's Institute leapt into the fray, and organized 3,500 local centres where 'jam-wives' could do their work on a national voluntary basis and save sugar, fruit – and their jam-making pride.

Perhaps the most impressive aspect of the women who lived in the country during World War Two was their bravery. This bravery expressed itself in many different ways, from defiance to resignation, but it seems to have been one of the tacit qualities that gave these women their heroic stature. It also makes conscientious objectors like Frances Partridge seem somehow diminished in comparison. Her principles were of course perfectly respectable, but the tone of her wartime diaries, as she observes the deprivations and tragedies going on around her, has a complacency and remoteness that was quite alien to the majority of her fellow-countrywomen, who chose to regard Hitler's work as the antics of a fool. When a bomb fell and damaged the table in the dining room of one country mansion, the butler was called to restore it at once so His Lordship might not be disturbed by 'that dreadful man'. Author Dorothy Black compared the bombing to a mosquito cruising around. 'Only the mosquito, instead of gnawing a limb, drops heavy eggs around.' Mrs Black was caught in one of the worst raids on Liverpool while she was in her bath. 'I arose, put on my tin hat and returned to my bath, a sweet sight – but one must wash.'

'One must wash.' Precisely. One must keep up standards. 'The garden fete season goes whizzing on,' blithely announced Bridget Chetwynd to *Tatler* readers in 1941. 'And the shrill cries of hoop-la addicts and bowlers for the pig echo round the walls of vicarage and manor house gardens, pianos tinkle against the often windy open air while schoolchildren dance and mime, the village postmistress crouches in a small tent wearing something brought back from the East by someone and tells fortunes . . . So the admirably light-hearted English demonstrate intact morale, and raise money for War Weapons . . .' (Fund-raising for war weapons was a constant activity. One tiny village of 700 residents, without the patronage of a large manor house, raised five thousand pounds in one week, with the happy result that an American, who read and was moved by the story, sent $50 to add to the kitty.)

Fashion writers urged their readers to maintain standards of style. To change or not to change – for dinner – that was the question. 'Those of us who have worked hardest know best how refreshing it is to change for dinner,' wrote Isabel Crampton in *Country Life,* showing a few suitable dinner dresses for wartime occasions. (This campaign was so successful that people snorted with delight when it was reported that Mussolini thought the English put on dinner jackets for tea.) Ladies required to wear uniforms were encouraged to have them properly tailored to fit, and to choose as good quality material as possible, to ensure a 'pleasant sartorial experience' when in uniform.

'I am finding that disturbed nights and sitting in shelters and journeys in crowded trains are making heavy inroads on my stock of lavender water,' complained another columnist, grateful to Yardley's for having thoughtfully introduced a purse-bottle in two sizes, priced at 1/6d and two shillings. But perhaps the most revealing story of keeping up appearances comes from Norman F. Ellison, a World War One veteran, who visited the elegant Jacobean house of some elderly friends for tea one afternoon. The butler brought in a priceless silver tray set with silver teapot, etc., and placed it calmly and sedately on an occasional table. 'Then I noticed the effect of wartime rationing on this delightful household. The jam was in its original pot, the margarine in its wrapper, the uncut loaf on a platter. My charming hostess explained. "Mr Churchill says we are wasting food. Every time jam is put on a plate it is not scraped clean; bread-and-butter not eaten is not put on the table a second time. So just take what you need." '

Bravery also manifested itself in the kind of amateurism that informs so many aspects of the British character. During the period when an invasion was expected at any minute, one elderly lady prepared herself for the German parachutists (who would surely arrive either very early, or very late, when the light was bad), by making ready a hairbrush, which she planned to point out of the window and bluff the invaders into mistaking it for a revolver. This sort of vague approach to the enemy was not restricted to elderly ladies. During a night raid a German airman was shot down at dusk over a rural part of England. Alone, and scared that in his flying suit someone would shoot him out of hand, he was desperate to find a police station where he might give himself up. Striking a country road, he met a soldier going home. Petrified, he tried to hide, but the soldier merely said, 'Good night,' and walked on. He then reached the gates of a level-crossing. A sleepy gatekeeper called to him to wait a minute, then came down, let him through and went back to bed. By this time the young German was in a complete panic and it was another twenty minutes before he found anyone who would take him seriously and arrest him.

This is not to say that people did not care what happened. Feeling for the countryside had probably never run higher. Rebecca West, writing a long article in a December 1940 issue of *The New Yorker* about the difficulties of doing up a country house in wartime, declared: 'I feel deeply about this house. I love some of the pictures and embroideries and carvings in my flat in London, but if they are bombed tomorrow I shall not feel any poignant grief. But if the Germans burn my farm buildings or machine-gun my cows, then I shall know real fury. I look at my haystack and grit my teeth at the thought of an incendiary bomb falling anywhere near it.'

The origin of her disaffection for possessions sprang from the war itself, from its devastating effect on the civilized world. 'We have a Rembrandt drawing, a minute, cunning, loving piece of magic, a few strokes of a pencil which show, receding into an immense distance, mile upon mile of Holland. We have a Dufy that shows Burgundy as it is after the vines have been sprayed with copper sulphate, a blue land, deep bright blue, delphinium blue. They have become portraits of enslaved countries, unvisitable, dangerous.'

The British countryside, however, was still unravished, although listening to bombs became a customary experience for all country dwellers. From the south and throughout the centre of England, the German planes flew over in wave upon wave, aiming for their selected targets. At Rodmell, Virginia Woolf recorded: 'They came very close. We lay down under the tree. The sound was like someone sawing the air just above us. We lay flat on our faces, hands behind head. Don't close your teeth, said Leonard ... Then slowly the sound lessened. Mabel in kitchen said the windows shook. Air raid still on: distant planes ... The all clear 5 to 7. 144 [planes] down last night.' And a young woman in Littlehampton wrote to a friend 'Many a night mother and I sat under the stairs listening to the German planes circling overhead and the bombs dropping in the distance. I used to try to read but kept reading the same page. I also tried to knit but found in the morning it was all a muddle.'

Those words speak poignantly of courage under duress. Often the women were very lonely, their loved ones far away and likely to be killed. It was a manless world. Sometimes billeted soldiers came to their rescue; others were victims of soldiers' unwelcome advances. Author Ronald Fraser's mother, beautiful and bored, succumbed to the attractions of a Wing Commander who was billeted on her. (She had been warned. The Wing Commander had originally been billeted on the local doctor, who threw him out because of his overtures to the doctor's wife.) Romances spring up quickly in a war. Emotions run high. Life is cheap. Women left behind are always vulnerable.

Humour was the best revenge. When invasion fears were at their height, rumours that the Germans were going to arrive dressed as clergymen or nuns caused everyone a great deal of amusement. Shopfront jokes took people's minds off things. After a particularly damaging air raid, a barber's shop sign read: WE HAD A CLOSE SHAVE. LET US GIVE YOU ONE. A chemist came up with: OUR PANES HAVE GONE. COME IN AND LET US REMOVE YOURS. Another sign announced: MORE OPEN THAN USUAL. In one country town, German planes dropped bombs on market day, and two bullets landed on the tray of a fishmonger's scale. They hit a codfish, and the fishmonger commented, 'If the price hadn't been fixed I could have sold it for double in souvenir steaks!'

This was nonchalance as a fine art, a stylized form of humour that was the chief characteristic of those sitting out the war in the increasingly threatened countryside. Vita Sackville-West described an incident that took place at Sissinghurst in 1940 which perhaps expresses most vividly the spirit of the times.

'We had just counted a third wave of forty bombers and fighters roaring past, leaving white streamers like the wake of ships across the blue. "Please, madam," said a quiet voice, "would you like luncheon out of doors? Then you could watch the fights better."'

Invasion of
Strangers

DURING THE SECOND WORLD WAR, approximately half a million foreign troops were billeted in Britain. This figure rose to at least one and a half million in late 1944, when the Normandy landings took place. They came from all over the world, but mostly, and most prominently, they came from the United States of America. A large number of these young fighting men were billeted in English country houses.

The invasion from across the Atlantic, while giving an immeasurable boost to the British war effort, created an unprecedented stir in almost every part of the countryside. Many of the locals had never seen an American before, except perhaps glamourized to an unreal degree in the cinema. Were all Americans like Clark Gable and John Wayne? For a while, anyway, it seemed so. They brought with them enthusiasm, new technology, their own drinking water in tins, it was said, being fearful of the home-grown variety, and most relevant of all at that time in ration-book Britain – food. Sugar, chocolate, cigarettes, liquor – all the items one most longs for during times of stress – the Americans handed out with a kind of reckless abandon that enchanted the grateful recipients.

Major C. S. Jarvis, author of A Countryman's Notes in *Country Life* during that time, waxed lyrical about other aspects of these new and marvellous creatures who had taken over the land. 'A little detail is the wonderful clearance of their Army vehicles,' he noted. 'Once I was driving on a slightly rough Welsh track, over which an American model would soar like a bird, when a dull thud followed by a complete disappearance of ignition, spark and every form of electricity, disclosed the fact that the battery of the car was lying in pieces of scrap on the road behind me.' Major Jarvis also commented with interest on the great variety of caps and headdresses the Americans possessed, 'so that the selection of the right one for the particular weather of the day must be a matter of some moment'.

Americans offered less obscure attractions than headgear to the younger members of the community. Apart from their gifts of luxurious groceries, they also seemed brasher, more confident and exciting than the local talent – what there was left of it, most able-bodied males having long gone to the war. Novels have been written, and films made, about the romantic liaisons that were struck up between GIs and English girls during those emotionally fraught wartime years. And it was not just the enlisted men either. Frances Partridge remembers Julia Strachey visiting Ham Spray and making them all laugh 'with her scintillating stories about the sexual approaches of American officers to the upper-class ladies of Chilton Foliat'. It seems there was some justification for the disgruntled phrase that went around at the time, 'The trouble with Americans is that they are over-paid, over-fed, over-sexed and over here.'

If the natives were disturbed by this dramatic new feature of local life, for the Americans it was indeed another country. Many of them arrived after long and debilitating troopship crossings of the Atlantic, some never having been to Europe before, let alone to a remote country spot where nobody ever showered and no restaurant had ever heard of a hamburger. They were billeted in huge country houses, many without central heating or hot water, to which they somehow had to adjust while preparing for an unknown adventure abroad in which they might well lose their lives.

'I was a combat photographer in the 386th Medium Bomb Group of the 9th US Army Air Force based on the estate of Lady Warwick called Easton Lodge, in Great Dunmow, Essex,' recalls William N. Scanlan. 'Our planes were Martin B26 Bombers, the same ones once characterized by the wartime Truman Commission as "flying prostitutes" because they seemed to have no visible means of support from their very short wingspans.

'Our photo section operated a laboratory and were billeted in a Nissen hut on the estate in a grove of very tall trees, hemlock I think, which were the home of hundreds of ravens. We enjoyed a magnificent frontal view of the Great House with its ivied façade. Accommodations within the Great House were not great, much of the interior having been allowed to deteriorate, but our people installed a few showers in what was apparently a wing of the house that had been used as a carriage house. There was no hot water and the facility was crude and quite gloomy. But going to London for a shower was not convenient and we made use of what we had.'

The Group Chaplain had quarters over this improvised shower area and was most unhappy to be subjected to the profane utterances of airmen suddenly deluged with icy water showers. 'So bodies were blue; the air was blue; but there was general cleanliness all round. "Deo gratias" said the Chaplain on these occasions as he matched our blue language with his own.'

(The hunt for a good shower seems to have preoccupied many of the US visitors. 'I showered in the Jockeys' Tack Room in Cheltenham,' confessed an intelligence officer working at Bletchley.)

Not many country houses seem to have come up to scratch for a nation used to better creature comforts. GIs were detailed to lay plumbing pipes at Walcot Hall, for instance, a Jacobean house near Stamford, in Lincolnshire. 'We were not allowed to use the fireplaces in the house,' Colonel John B. B. Trussell remembers. 'So we were miserably cold. The US had brought in Sibley stoves to warm the rooms, but there were so many troops in tents that their need was regarded as greater than ours and the stoves were taken away. The horrors of war meant to us to be forced out of bed in the middle of the night . . .'

The owner of Walcot Hall was not thrilled by the plumbing pipes or the hundreds of Americans milling about in his world-famous Italian gardens, which the locals said had cost a quarter of a million pounds and needed fourteen gardeners. When the Colonel requested permission to shoot doves on the estate, it was denied. 'My little property has already suffered too much the ravages of war,' the owner was rumoured to have said. (The ravages were not always the responsibility of the foreigners, however. Americans noticed that on many occasions, the houses they took over from the British had already suffered considerable damage – doorknobs pulled off, mouldings broken, interiors disintegrating and filled with the debris of operations rooms, maps, charts, and the paraphernalia of war.)

The incongruity of some of the billets seems curious now. James Fechheimer, a sergeant attached to the 2nd Squadron, 102nd Cavalry (the federalized Essex Troop of the New Jersey National Guard), was stationed for a few months in 1942 at Faringdon House in Berkshire, the home of Lord Berners. 'There was no sign of Lord Berners,' he recalls. 'Just his Rolls-Royce in the stable row. I remember being quite impressed by the fact that there was a private entrance from his garden into the yard of Faringdon Church.' Nor was there any sign of the famous doves, which was probably fortunate. What American GIs would have thought of dyed pink and yellow birds cooing in the garden defies description. The only oddity about the house was that the cupola on the roof with its golden ball was swathed in rugs to prevent it being a landmark to the Germans in the moonlight. Lady Harrod remembers staying at Faringdon in the war with her two small sons. 'One of the beautiful four-poster beds was in the drawing room and Henry and Dominic had to sleep in it and I was terrified they would wet it!' Although Berners was nervous about the arrival of the Americans, it became clear that their presence was a godsend, in terms of maintenance (keeping on the heating etc.), and like many owners, in the end he was grateful to them.

Mr Fechheimer was not billeted inside Faringdon itself, but in Nissen huts in the grounds, so he rarely got to see the elegant interior of the house. Staff Sergeant Alexander Nazemetz, an aerial gunner with the 100th Bomb Group, tells a different story. He was sent for a week's rest to Walhampton Park, Lymington, Hampshire, after flying twenty missions over occupied enemy territory in 1944. This house was not like the others; it served as a respite for enlisted men who had endured particularly dangerous combat duty. 'Rather than turn us loose, they told us to go there.' Staff Sergeant Nazemetz loved it. 'We were treated royally (compared to regular army air force). We had breakfast, lunch, tea, dinner and a late snack. We were awakened by a butler who also served orange juice ... We were issued civilian clothes. We also had bikes for local touring – and for beating out Mother England from a halfpenny toll across a bridge into Lymington where we occasionally sojourned for a quick scotch (served only between 9 and 9.15 pm).'

He also celebrated his twentieth birthday there. Far from home, briefly absent from the death zone, he wrote letters to his family about Walhampton, with a kind of cheerful awe: 'It is very old in architecture and has a grand staircase just off to the left-hand side ... There is a large hallway with a railing that overlooks the spacious room below ... The terrace is positively enormous and the lawn that requires several men working steadily is in fair shape even now in February. And what 1700 home is complete without at least two or three fountains to brighten up the lawns? All of them have bronze figures of Mercury, etc. Today it was quite nice out so we took some pictures and I hope that they come out. Course Mom may not appreciate the ones where we are standing next to a completely nude figure whose sculptor must have been a very broadminded man.'

Organized activities at Walhampton kept the men's minds off their nightmares. A dance took place with Englishwomen in uniform. There was a badminton tournament, and a boxing match with boys from the village. Then the week was over and Staff Sergeant Nazemetz returned to combat. He now lives in New Jersey, survivor of thirty-three flying missions into Europe.

Pylewell Park, a couple of miles from Walhampton, was also a base for Americans, and while not reserved like Walhampton for R & R, seems to have inspired the same kind of feeling in its temporary residents. Joseph Lynch, who was working with the British on the Enigma Code, spent two happy months at Pylewell in 1943. 'You felt on top of the world, aware of the building and what it must have been like in peacetime. I was nineteen years old, and lived in Jersey City. I didn't know what roses were really. Going into the garden was a fantastic experience. For the first time I found myself living close to nature.'

Cliveden also offered respite in a special way. The Astors offered Cliveden to the Government in 1939, and eighty-three child evacuees arrived in the first week of the war. They were eventually housed on the estate while the house, which had been a Canadian hospital in World War One, once again opened its doors to the Canadian Forces. A hospital was built on the polo grounds, and the staff and medical personnel were billeted in a wing of the house, with overflow in gardeners' cottages and at nearby Taplow House.

The interior of Cliveden was largely untouched during the war, most of the paintings, including a collection of Reynoldses, remaining on the walls, and only the most valuable items such as the Orkney tapestries being removed. This was because the Astors continued to live in the house, and took an active interest in their wartime guests that was much appreciated by the Canadian officers and patients.

Lord Astor, like many large house-owners, was anxious about the future, and by 1942 had already embarked on negotiations to make over Cliveden to the National Trust. According to James Lees-Milne, the endowment was to be £200,000, the hospital in the grounds adding another £3,000 to £4,000 a year. He shared the hope of many owners who had constructed hospitals on estate grounds that the hospital would continue to be used in the post-war period – at a substantial rental. In most cases, this did not work out. (The financial details were long in negotiation with the Trust, and the house was finally open to the public for the first time in 1948.)

But while Lord Astor was thus preoccupied, Lady Astor involved herself in the affairs of the Canadian visitors with typical energy and enthusiasm. 'Lady Astor herself was in residence and took quite an interest in our organization and almost daily visited some part of the hospital,' says Dr R. G. Lea, a medical officer attached to the hospital. 'These visits were always riotous, hilarious affairs – very funny and lively. The boys, with nothing better to do, would carefully follow the goings-on in the House of Commons and would be prepared for her, and she would enter into the spirit very willingly. One day the boys read that Aneurin Bevan had referred to her as "an old windbag," and that was good for a night's hilarity. She was a Christian Scientist, but at no time did she ever attempt to interfere. She used, however, to leave Christian Science pamphlets on the beds as she went around and I would follow her, pick them up and as she left, hand them back. This never failed to get the expected reaction out of her and she certainly supplied the patients with many a lively evening.'

Dr Lea and some of his colleagues were sometimes invited to the Big House for meals. 'I recall one day at lunch the centrepiece of the table was composed of a large and very beautiful assortment of fresh fruit. Having seen nothing of that nature since leaving Canada, we were eager to get at it, but towards the end of the meal, Lady Astor told the butler to put it away, it was for a later meal and we had had enough! I recall too, a dance she held in the Great Hall for all our "other ranks". It was a very festive occasion. Lady Astor herself danced the very vigorous dances of the day without flagging. I cannot recall where she managed to line up any girls for the party, but they were there.

'On another occasion she called to one of our officers to come up and meet some guests on a Sunday afternoon. He was rather abashed to discover himself in the company of many of the mighty figures of our time and quickly took refuge in a far corner of the Hall where he had a very pleasant afternoon talking to two very nice teenage girls. He enquired of one of them what her name was and she replied Elizabeth Cavendish [the daughter of the Duke of Devonshire]. When he asked the other what her name was, she said "Elizabeth," and had no other name. This, of course, was our present Queen.'

Lady Astor's role at Cliveden is all the more impressive considering that she was still Member of Parliament for Plymouth, and spent her time shuttling to and from her beleaguered constituency. A somewhat less favourable note is struck by the story told by the black American Secretary of the NAACP, Walter White, who visited Cliveden in 1944. White was a very light-skinned black, and on seeing him, Nancy Astor exclaimed, 'You're an idiot! You are an idiot calling yourself a Negro when you're whiter than I am, with blue eyes and blond hair!' She then added insult to injury by telling him after lunch, 'We never have any trouble with the good black boys, it's the near-white ones who cause the trouble. They're always talking about and insisting on rights.'

The experiences of black American soldiers in Britain is the subject of a book by Graham Smith entitled *When Jim Crow Met John Bull*. He describes the situation at Wortley Hall, the estate of Lord Wharncliffe, as symbolizing the confusion and conflict that the black occupation caused. Wortley Hall had been requisitioned by the Air Ministry and had been turned over to the American Army Air Force in 1942. White troops occupied part of Wortley Hall, while the blacks were quartered in tents in the grounds. (The US still practised segregation at that time, of course.) 'In their off-duty activities the black GIs were having a good time. They had "considerable relationships" with local girls and those from Sheffield. Prostitutes and factory girls came from there in taxis to be paid for their favours in money or rations. All "actively solicited" black soldiers.' While the police attempted to break up these activities by arresting some of the women, there seems to have been only minimal concern. Indeed one police inspector stated that 'the people in this community had no prejudice against coloured soldiers because they were coloured.'

Although the colour problem was a very small aspect of the war in England, it deeply affected the country areas where negro soldiers were based. We are now accustomed to a multi-racial world, but in those days the influx of black faces in village shops and pubs, let alone country houses, was both exotic and unnerving. The truth was that many English people simply didn't know how to deal with them. All sorts of advice was forthcoming. In the *Sunday Pictorial* of 6 September 1942, for instance, an article quoted the advice of the wife of the vicar of Worle, near Weston-super-Mare, who told her parishioners that shopkeepers might serve the black soldiers but to tell them not to come again, while ladies should move, if seated next to them in a cinema. After some more of this sort of thing, including the advice that 'on no account must coloured troops be invited into the homes of white women', the newspaper added cheerfully, 'Any coloured soldier who reads this may rest assured that there is no colour bar in this country and that he is as welcome as any other Allied soldier.'

This ambivalence was experienced by all social classes. Frances Penrose related a story to Frances Partridge and her pacifist friends about an American officer's lecture to the local ladies about how to treat the blacks. They were told to beware of any friendly impulse towards them, never let them into their houses, and above all never treat them as human beings, because they were not. 'Frances said that the faces of the ladies were a study in delighted horror, as they heard that none of their daughters' virginities were safe and that all the blacks carried knives. "How are the poor blacks to be entertained?" asked one brave lady. "Oh, you needn't worry about that. They are always happy, and make their own entertainment by singing and laughing." ' When James Lees-Milne saw 600 negro troops at Montacute, he commented cautiously, as though about aliens from outer space, 'They smile and say "Hello" in an engaging manner.'

Edward Laper, an American with the 680th Engineer Topographic Company, stationed at Harefield Hall in Wilmslow, Cheshire, remembers being told that if they saw black GIs with white girls, that was OK in England. But tensions mounted. Racial violence between American blacks and whites began to be reported in the newspapers, and sexual assaults and criminality became more and more commonplace in the small villages of England where blacks were billeted. Furthermore, it was quite clear that local girls found the black soldiers irresistible, and stories of their extraordinary sexual prowess spread through the countryside. The inevitable result of this was an epidemic of what were called 'brown babies', provoking the Conservative Member of Parliament for Penryn in Cornwall, Maurice Petherick, to ask the Foreign Office in 1943 whether the Foreign Secretary could 'arrange with the American Government to send [the blacks] to North Africa, or to go and fertilize the Italians who are used to it anyhow'.

(How serious the problem actually was can be seen in the results of a survey carried out in 1945 by Sylvia McNeill for the League of Coloured Peoples. It reported that up to that year 553 brown babies had been born to 545 mothers, of whom 92 were married and 98 were unmarried (the status of the rest was unknown). County by county, the numbers read, for instance, Gloucestershire 60, Cornwall 38, Devon 83, Hampshire 50, Suffolk 34, Lancashire 70 – these being places heavily populated by black troops.)

There is no doubt that the exposure of the British to large numbers of American blacks forced them to consider, probably for the first time, the problems of racism, and while many enjoyed the company of the 'black Yanks', post-war attitudes towards immigration were to some extent formed during those years of the war when approximately 130,000 blacks were billeted in Britain.

Americans and Canadians were not the only foreigners on British soil, of course. Refugees from Europe came in large numbers, hoping to find work for themselves and schools for their children. Irene Schmied came from Germany and found herself in quite a considerable country house, Yattendon Court, Lord Iliffe's estate in Yattendon, Berkshire, which had been requisitioned for Winceby House School, a small institution whose registration went up after it moved into its rather elegant wartime quarters! 'I was fourteen years old,' Ms Schmied says, 'and I remember the huge hall with a big fireplace where we had dancing classes. We were not allowed to use the tennis courts or go into the woods. Lord Iliffe lived in the village and used to keep an eye on the place. Our headmistress was always telling me to walk straight, like a pine or an oak. "I hope you'll remember," she said, "that you went to school in one of the stately homes of England." '

Ronald Fraser describes the experiences of Nelly, arriving from Vienna to work for his mother at the Manor House, Amnersfield, in 1940. Mrs Fraser seems to have been less troubled than most by the stringent rationing, according to the new cook. Lunch was extensive. 'Soup, meat, two vegetables, fruit and cheese. Madam loved goulash, schnitzels, dumplings, salads, mayonnaise ... The larder was full of fruit I had bottled. One day she came in with some cherries. What a shame we haven't got sugar to bottle these, she say to me. I take her to the cupboard and show her the 40 lbs of sugar we got there. She didn't know. It come from the parcels her mother send from America. You wouldn't know there was a war. When I was in Vienna still, I was thinking so often that in England my child will go hungry. But never, never in the Manor House. We got everything ...'

Images of the foreign invasion remain. There is John Lehmann's picture of American GIs at Stonehenge, 'wandering in and out of the rings, or nonchalantly lying against the trilithons, chewing gum'. There is the ghost of a Canadian soldier, accidentally shot on the stairs of Hammerwood Park, near East Grinstead, which still haunts the house. There is Lord Cobham's story about the American officer who, on being shown the Vandyke painting of the Descent from the Cross at Hagley, pointed to the figure of Our Lord and said, 'Who was that guy that looked sick?' And there is William Scanlan, with a photographer's eye, describing the bittersweet, almost mystical experiences of his time at Lady Warwick's estate at Easton. 'In the evenings, we'd often lie on our backs on the lawn in front of Warwick Castle, as we called it, watching the aerial dogfights as the RAF faced the Luftwaffe ... The endless raven conversations at night mixed eerily with the grinding engine sounds of German bombers on their way to London.'

Easton Lodge is gone now. Lady Warwick's ancient gabled house and garden, with its pergolas and herbaceous borders, and the park she turned into an animal kingdom, were all razed by the RAF, and now a family lives in what was left of the main building. Traces of the American occupation remain. The wading pool in the garden is where the notorious freezing makeshift showers were located. Mr Scanlan went back in 1952 to look, as did hundreds of American enlisted men and officers after the war was over. They still do, even now – returning to the English country houses that for a brief and extraordinary period belonged to them.

Some, like Easton Lodge, no longer stand. Others remain, but have fallen on hard times. A few are just the same. Walhampton Park was fortunate, and became a school after the war. Pylewell is still in private hands. Visiting these two houses now, situated in splendour overlooking the Solent, both with glorious gardens sloping gently down to the water, one can imagine the calming effect they must have had on the young men from American cities and towns, who found themselves transported for a fleeting moment from the bombs and guns into these serene and timeless landscapes.

Lights On

ON 16 August 1945, Norman Ellison, like thousands of his fellow-countrymen, celebrated the end of the war. 'At night we went to Caldy Hill to see the bonfires blazing on the distant Welsh hills. What pleased us more was to see the opposite side of the Dee twinkling with thousands of street lamps and lighted windows. So we went home, opened wide the curtains and switched on every light in the house. More than anything else did this action, taken by nearly everyone, bring home to us the fact that the war had ended.'

The euphoria of these rural communities, needless to say, did not last long. While many lights went on, many others had been turned off for good. Oddly enough, bombs and rockets were not the major sources of devastation, in spite of German reports that certain British landmarks had been targeted for destruction. The threats were real enough, to be sure. 'Our art connoisseurs know the English Baedeker thoroughly. They know where all the historic Tudor houses are, the exact position of Canterbury Cathedral, where the spas are situated, and most of the famous castles and homes of the nobility. Our airmen will know how to find and hit them.' But the so-called Baedeker Raids were remarkably unsuccessful, at least insofar as country houses were concerned. Mount Edgcumbe in Cornwall was gutted by incendiary bombs during an attack on Plymouth; Knole, Penshurst, Lamb House were some of those badly hurt. Many had light damage. But the real damage could not be placed at the door of the Germans.

For the most part, the mopping-up period after 1945 was probably one of the more disheartening aspects of the war for many country house-owners.

When war was declared Lady Dunsany said that to her and everyone else the first priority was that, whatever the cost, we must defeat the Germans. But once that had been achieved, the golden glow of victory was dimmed in the face of harsh economic and social reality.

Lady Dunsany's story is typical. Her family owned three large houses situated in West Wales, considered to be one of the safest areas in the country. Therefore they were all requisitioned shortly after the outbreak of war. Her mother had recently died in a house called Tregegb. This was taken over by a girls' school from the east coast of England. Fortunately the old housekeeper was allowed to stay on and to act as matron and as she had a strong personality she saw that little damage was done – the pupils kept up the vegetable garden and although the lawns became meadows the paths were kept weeded.

Lady Dunsany had married Baron de Rutzen in 1932. As he was on the reserve list of the Welsh Guards he was called up immediately and after a few months his regiment was sent to North Africa and from thence to Italy and sadly he never saw his home again. Baron de Rutzen owned Slebech Park, an eighteenth-century castellated mansion. It was requisitioned by the Army, and left in the care of some regular officers as a centre for conscientious objectors whose work there was to install a pipeline to bring water to the increasing population coming to that area. This particular combination of regular officers and enlisted ranks was disastrous; it could scarcely prove otherwise – personal hostility between the mainly intellectual pacifists and the military often verged on violence and the house suffered in consequence. It had been difficult to find accommodation for all the contents. Many of the larger paintings and mirrors had been boarded-up and left in their rooms – some of these were stolen or damaged beyond repair, the floors and walls left in a deplorable condition and the castellations were vandalized leaving the house with a derelict appearance.

Picton Castle, the home Lady Dunsany really loved, belonged to her brother, Sir John Philipps. This magnificent house was also requisitioned by the Army for a convalescent home and the Park was used as a large training-camp covered with tents and Nissen huts. Sir John had not been passed fit for active service. He was allowed to keep a flat at Picton as he had a large estate and home-farm to look after, his land agent having been called up. He also had a flat in London, having business interests there.

Sir John had a gregarious personality and so enjoyed the company of all the officers and men making for a happy and congenial atmosphere in Picton. An old laundry, which was very damp, was used to house some of the contents of the Castle so some of the furniture suffered badly; surprisingly, very little was stolen but the gardens and grounds were wrecked. There had been no time to make proper inventories of the contents or of the state of these three houses so it was difficult to get any adequate compensation. Lady Dunsany, having only one child, a daughter, was working all through the war – first for the *Daily Sketch* War Relief Fund, then at a bomb factory outside Glasgow, and finally for the Ministry of Supply. She did try to get to Wales for weekends and to see her only daughter in the holidays but said she was always too disheartened to visit Slebech.

Her husband was killed in Italy just before the war ended so she felt her personal loss was so much greater than the devastation caused to Slebech that the latter seemed relatively unimportant. The house was uninhabitable, so, when in Wales, she lived with her brother in Picton until he died suddenly in 1948.

Lady Dunsany re-married and went to live in Ireland. Tregegb has continued as a school. Slebech and Picton were sold to two distant relatives who have spent a great deal of money and care in restoring them to the beautiful houses they are today.

The destruction of paintings, furniture, windows, floors, roofs is immediately apparent, but damp, dry rot and decay are insidious vandals, taking their toll slowly and irrevocably. Langholm Lodge, in Dumfriesshire, one of the Duke of Buccleuch's houses, was one such victim. Langholm was wholly occupied by the Army, and when one lot of troops moved out there was sometimes a gap of a few weeks before the next moved in. 'It appeared to be the custom of the Army to wash down the decks as if they were on board ship, so that the combination of frequent flooding and lack of airing led to rampant dry rot activity.' (This seafaring approach to country living is confirmed by a Canadian enlisted man who was billeted at an estate near Petersfield where, he says, 'after the fashion of the Royal Navy it was called as if a ship, and I think it was HMS *Mercury*.') Unluckily, the Duke recalls, this treatment did not manifest itself until some time after compensation had been settled. When efforts were made to tackle the dreaded affliction, it had progressed so far that it was impossible to save the house. 'It was a charming, plain Georgian house, which would most certainly have been a listed building under today's conservation procedures.'

As early as 1942, there had been a debate in the House of Commons on the vexed subject of damage caused by army occupation of country houses. In the discussion, a former housemaster at Cheltenham averred that the 150 troops who had lived under his own roof 'compared favourably in their conduct as members of the Army with the public schoolboys who were members of my house'. But soldiers are not angels, though airmen may have wings, as a jaundiced commentator remarked, and most people's experience was less favourable. Emily Hahn, returning to her husband's country house in Dorset in 1946, describes what must have been a typical scene for returning house-owners: dirty walls, splintered wood, grime, every porcelain washbasin smashed, plumbing broken. Only the metal bathtubs had resisted the Army, as she put it, being metal. The local agent told them to leave everything as desolate as they could. 'Don't do a thing until you're sure they'll pay you for what they've damaged.' This advice, of course, was totally unrealistic. Ms Hahn and her husband set to work, as anybody would, to try and clean the place up and make it habitable, while waiting in vain for the Army to come and give an estimate.

In 1946 the writer Denton Welch visited a church in Kent in which soldiers had been billeted. All over the walls he saw pictures of girls drawn in chalk, with enormous breasts, little pants, frizzy hair. 'I pictured the grim dormitory.' If soldiers were the main culprits in causing damage to houses, it must be remembered that in many cases these were young, inexperienced men, far from home, waiting to be called to action from which they might never return. If they looked around them at all, they saw, not beautiful antique bannisters or glorious eighteenth-century mouldings, but grim dormitories, the precincts of death.

Human occupation was not the only cause of mistreatment. In some cases houses were requisitioned but never occupied, thus being left vacant for years at a time, vulnerable to burst pipes, dry rot, dilapidation, vandalism, the usual casualties of an empty house. There were also less visible abuses. At the outbreak of war, on the existing scale of death duties, two deaths in one decade (obviously no longer out of the question) were sufficient to break up almost any estate. The Death Duties Act of 1940 to some extent remedied this punishing state of affairs by remitting death duties on property changing hands more than once owing to death in action. But in 1945, taxation on real property remained at an oppressively high level, and death duties continued to compel executors to throw all sorts of freeholds and leaseholds on to the market.

The litany of war damage to country houses started almost as soon as the first occupations took place and continued long after the war officially ended in 1945. While house-owners were permitted to apply for compensation as soon as the damage occurred, in many cases the compensation was inadequately estimated and inadequately paid for. In his memoir *Two Exiles,* the headmaster of Malvern College, H. C. A. Gaunt, goes into some detail about the frustrations and obstacles encountered in the exercise of the Compensation (Defence) Act of 1939, which, as he says, was drawn up with industrial and commercial establishments in mind, 'and without proper regard to the position and needs of schools and certain other similar institutions'. Broadly speaking, its provisions were that a fair rent should be paid for requisitioned buildings, based on the rent which in August 1939 might have been expected, if the buildings had been rented to another occupier. In addition the expenses caused by removal, e.g. such things as transport, storage and out-of-pocket expenses, should also be paid. 'This,' says Mr Gaunt, 'seems a not unreasonable arrangement.' But he goes on to point out that schools find it hard to estimate a rent for a property that has no obvious rentable market value. Moreover most of the schools involved were non-profit organizations; and furthermore, there were far more expenses involved in, say, moving Malvern to Blenheim, than merely the cost of transport. (See page 77 for further details of this case.)

Private house-owners came up against similar problems. The forms alone were complicated and obscure. The bureaucratic procedures involved in making the application were debilitating. Diana Brinton-Lee records a visit to the War Damage Department before the war ended: 'When I got there I could not find it at first, but I discovered it at last, appropriately housed in an abandoned underground air-raid shelter in a patch of waste ground. Here a lot of young women were working at trestle tables on kitchen chairs, and the humble ratepayers who had committed the impropriety of being bombed were waiting patiently in queues.'

Materials were in desperately short supply, particularly the kinds of materials required for the interiors of the older houses. Where was one going to get damask, or marble, or stained glass? Pre-war inventories were made in a hurry, or made under pressure of immediate occupation. Many valuables were simply not recorded, and thus inapplicable for compensation. As for the exteriors of houses, the financial restrictions were in many cases tantamount to prohibition. James Lees-Milne described in his diary the case of a National Trust property, Aylsham Old Hall in Norfolk. 'The army have de-requisitioned it, and given us £450 for dilapidations, out of which we are allowed to spend £100 if the work is undertaken before 1 August. After that date only £10 pa is allowed, which means that no one can possibly inhabit large houses after troops have been billeted in them for six years.'

Another serious obstacle to exterior repair was the unusually strict building restrictions that owners were faced with even if they had the energy, optimism and bank account to embark on restoration. To do any kind of building, licences had to be obtained from the Ministry of Works, and were only granted under the strictest conditions. These licences had originated as wartime measures to prevent unnecessary use of valuable labour and materials, but after the war it was felt that in the new Labour Party mood of austerity, these restrictions should be maintained, so that only the most basic, practical construction could take place. While war damage entitled a house-owner to a licence more easily than if he wished to add, embellish, or build anew, and while various house-owners got round the red tape anyway, the restrictions minimized restoration. Some individuals, such as Earl Peel at Hyning Hall, and the Duke of Bedford's staff at Woburn, were prosecuted and convicted for unlawful remodelling.

The estates of the country houses also faced ruin. Some estate farmers, forced by wartime conditions to operate their agricultural land under official guidelines, found that in the post-war period the ploughed-up land could not be as profitably worked. Aerodromes, Nissen huts, bomb and rifle practice areas, munitions dumps, landmines, radio and telephone installations, had all taken their toll on the once-beautiful parklands that were so inextricably a part of the country house landscape. Irreplaceable trees had been felled, follies and fountains vandalized. James Lees-Milne describes the hacking of the sarcophagus at Blickling 'with a blunt instrument', and the carving of Canadian troops' names and addresses on the James Paine Bridge at Brocket Hall, 'all complete and inches deep'. Gardens were overgrown and valuable plants lost (some of Exbury's famous azaleas strangled by nettles and brambles, for instance), lawns turned into wildernesses, driveways churned up by tanks, fences down, shrubberies destroyed.

But requisitioning was not always the disaster it was made out to be. Damage was not invariably destructive. At Ripley Castle, for instance, after taking in children from Dr Barnardo's homes, 'our statue of Venus Emerging From the Bath was apparently improved by having its subject's toenails coloured green,' reports Sir Thomas Ingilby. Requisitioning in many cases helped, if not even saved some of the larger and more dilapidated properties. Owners, who could not afford to keep up their houses, suddenly found that their responsibilities were assumed by others. A small income could be gleaned by the rental of the property. The occupiers in many cases upgraded plumbing and heating systems. Central heating could be kept on at the occupiers' expense; maintenance of the house was attended to; damage from bombs or other enemy attacks was in some cases very quickly taken care of. Certain alterations of land for agricultural purposes, aerodromes or reconnaissance areas, helped improve the landscape by opening up vistas, removing old or dying trees, making use of fallow acres.

Perhaps the most important benefit came from the change in attitude towards the houses themselves. The owners of many of the bigger houses, often aristocrats in physical or economic decline, were forced by the time the war ended to face the fact that pre-war life with butlers, footmen and fine port in the cellar was gone for ever, and that their houses were under threat of extinction, if not by Hitler's bombs, then by the social realities of a post-war world. For a few, these realities were too much to bear, as in the much-quoted case of Lord and Lady Newton, owners of one of England's finest houses, Lyme Park. James Lees-Milne saw them on several occasions during nego- tiations for Lyme to be given to the National Trust. 'Both said they would never be able to reconcile themselves to the new order after the war. They admitted that their day was done, and life as they had known it was gone for ever. How right they are, poor people.' When he finally left Lyme for ever in 1946, Lord Newton sent a pathetic note of farewell to his staff in which he said, 'We are unwilling to depart and to end without a word the associations of five and a half centuries . . .'

But for all the Newtons, there were many more who resolved to seek new solutions to allow them to carry on the heavy burden of maintaining their family seats for posterity. In his book, *Old Money,* Nelson Aldrich describes the sense of uselessness and loss of social relevance experienced by those ordained to inherited wealth in the United States. It seems that the crisis of their ancient houses and traditional livelihoods provided the British equivalents with an invigorating and long-lasting *raison d'être.*

The National Trust was one solution. Lord Lothian, owner of Blickling Hall in Norfolk, saw the devastating future awaiting the great houses of Britain well before World War Two began. 'I do not think it an exaggeration,' he said in 1934, 'that within a generation, hardly one of these historic houses, save perhaps a few near London, will be lived in by the families who created them. Yet it is these 400 or 500 families who have for 300 or 400 years guided the fortunes of the nation.'

Lord Lothian's idea was to initiate a scheme whereby owners might bequeath their house and its contents to the National Trust, continuing, if they wished, to remain as life tenants, while from then on being exempt from death duties and taxation on the house or on as much of the estate as had been made over to the Trust as endowment. This scheme was embodied in the National Trust Act of 1937, with Lord Lothian taking the lead in making over Blickling to the Trust as the first house under the Act in 1940.

At first people were slow to follow Lord Lothian's example. The fledgling scheme was regarded by many with deep suspicion, not only because it seemed to be arrogating to itself the responsibilities more appropriately attaching to the landowners or even to the state, but also because it was perceived as hastening the demise of the privileged class to which most of the house-owners belonged. The notion of handing over one's estate to the Trust smacked of the treatment meted out to endangered species, whereby animals faced with extinction were killed and stuffed and presented to a museum – splendid for the museum, but not conducive to the perpetuation of the species.

But as the war progressed, thanks to the keen recruiting of James Lees-Milne and his colleagues, and to the examples of Lord Lothian, Lord Esher and other early supporters, who realized that this might be the only way to save their homes, the National Trust list of houses grew.

Another solution considered by house-owners was to turn their house into an institution – a school, a hotel, an agricultural training centre. This possibility was particularly attractive to owners whose houses had acted in a similar institutional capacity during the war. But difficulties arose almost immediately when such suggestions were proposed, including problems of staffing such institutions, many of which were situated in isolated rural spots, and equipping antiquated buildings efficiently enough to cope with large numbers of people and services. There was also a deep-seated resistance in the hearts and minds of many owners to the idea of their houses being forced to relinquish their role as family homes. In the middle of the war, when Brocket Hall was being used as a sanctuary for the City of London Maternity Hospital, whose building had been blitzed (well over 2,000 babies were born at Brocket), Lord Brocket declared that far from considering his house in the future being retained as an institution, 'I have every intention of living there once more, thus restoring to its proper use an historic English home.'

But the solution which had the most far-reaching consequences, and which has come to dominate the direction of country house survival into the next century, was to open the house to the public. The Marchioness of Exeter, writing in the November 1945 issue of *Country Life*, urged this on her fellow house-owners, warning that the alternative was for their houses to be closed for ever. She was driven to admit, however, that staff problems might well seem insurmountable. 'All I can do is say that owners, impoverished by taxation and increased costs as they are, desire to open their houses again to the public; that it is the houses and their irreplaceable contents that require the staff, not the personal needs of the owner-residents; and that if the country as a whole wishes its treasure houses to be maintained by their traditional and rightful guardians, not as museums but as homes with a soul and atmosphere – the result of loving care given by successive generations – the necessary assistance must be forthcoming somehow.'

In 1945 the prospect seemed daunting indeed. Building restrictions, shortage of materials, lack of staff, extremity of dilapidation, all conspired to present an almost insuperable hurdle to those owners who stood in their grounds after VJ Day and gazed up at their noble piles. In 1974 the Victoria and Albert Museum presented an exhibition entitled 'The Destruction of the Country House 1873–1973', in which some 1,400 houses were shown to have been destroyed during this century. The list was actually higher, and with the accompaniment of the grim growl of the bulldozer, the numbers brought home to the exhibition's many visitors the damning roll-call of lost treasures.

But the astonishing thing is that even though at least 400 houses were demolished after 1945, largely as a consequence of war damage, many more were in fact restored and brought back to life. Even the most faint-hearted dowager, gazing at her crumbling walls, broken windows, lost furniture, the horrendous wear-and-tear of licentious soldiery or incontinent orphans, seems to have summoned up the spirit of national tradition or personal pride vigorously enough to decide to move back in and start picking up the pieces. These efforts, fuelled by the knowledge that this time it was truly 'Do or Die', and aided in later years by more generous government grants, started a movement that has not abated since.

The public's increasing fascination for privately-owned treasures and treasure houses, and the ubiquitous fashion on both sides of the Atlantic for the so-called 'English Country House Look' in interior decorating (causing much mirth amongst the owners for whom 'decorating' means concealing the torn chintz with a cushion or hiding the hole in the wall with a picture), have resulted in the most enthusiastic revival in popularity of the great houses of Britain, so much so that a large part of the country's tourist industry depends on their continued existence.

When the late Margaret, Countess of Lichfield married her husband just after the war and moved into Shugborough Hall, she found the house badly damaged by the departed Army – the banisters of the main staircase, for instance, and a fine horseshoe table in the dining room, had been burned for firewood. The park had been taken over by the Americans for a hospital, and later for German prisoners-of-war. One day, when Lady Lichfield was walking around the temporary hospital buildings in the park with an army colonel, they discovered in one of the cavernous huts a row of coffins at one end, and a row of babies' cots at the other. The symbolism of this poignant sight did not escape her, and it seems a fitting image with which to end the story of how one world ended and another began.

THE
HOUSES

The School
LONGLEAT HOUSE

*'It will be something to tell my grandchildren
that I slept in the same room as the Duchess
of Kent.'*
– Schoolgirl's letter, 1940

Longleat House

WARMINSTER · WILTSHIRE

THE FIRST WORLD WAR was not kind to the Thynne family, owners of Longleat since 1540. The 5th Marquess of Bath's brother was killed in 1918, and his eldest son John, Viscount Weymouth, was killed in February 1916 on the Western Front, at the age of twenty. This gave the inheritance to the younger son, Henry, who remembers standing outside Longleat in 1916 (it was then a military hospital) wondering to himself, 'How can I look after you? I'll never be able to do it.'

When the Second War came, the 5th Marquess was seventy-seven years old. His wife, Violet, had died in 1928, and his two daughters were married. His son Henry was away at the war. (He had joined the Royal Wiltshire Regiment and was wounded in Palestine, after which he became British Liaison Officer to the American 19th Corps and served with them until the end of the war.) In 1937 Lord Bath, then living alone at Longleat, with some foresight had suggested to the Office of Works that the Royal School for Daughters of Officers of the Army, a girls' public school near Bath, should be given asylum at Longleat, since the school buildings, like those of Malvern College, had been earmarked by the Admiralty. This offer was a voluntary one. He neither asked for payment nor expected it. It was, as so often in those days, a 'gentleman's agreement', which was later to cause some difficulty.

In 1939 the Royal School (consisting of 300 girls and staff) moved in, or rather hurtled in, since the Admiralty had requested the school buildings to be vacated in forty-eight hours. This haste upset the housekeeper of Longleat, who was not prepared to receive the invasion of movers and organizers on her precious turf, and Lord Bath himself had to take charge. The house had been prepared to some extent, with the removal of valuable furniture and furnishings to the stables and chapel. Lord Bath kept only four rooms for himself. Lady Bath's rooms were turned into a sick bay. When the school arrived, the staff in residence consisted of one housekeeper, one cook, one butler, three laundry maids, three housemaids, one pantry lad, two motor men, and two odd-job men. This may sound a lot today, but compared to Longleat's *fin-de-siècle* heyday, when the household numbered over forty, this happy few remaining to look after 118 rooms represented quite a reduction.

The school's financial status *vis-à-vis* Longleat offers a typical case history of how country houses coped with requisitioning during those years. From 1939 to 1942, the school was able to operate successfully without paying a penny to Lord Bath. The school itself added temporary buildings, a shower bath block (there were only six bathrooms in the house!), and other sanitary, electrical heating and hot-water systems. But no rent or compensation whatsoever came to the old Marquess. His agent, Thomas B. Gill, urged him from time to time to impose certain charges, such as a proportion of rates and other maintenance charges, but His Lordship refused. Only in 1942 did Lord Bath go back to his agent, with the sad admission that he could no longer live on his income, and requesting help from the estate. Mr Gill once more said the school should do something, and as a result a rough memorandum was drawn up, listing expenses such as £1,000 per year for rental, plus additional annual expenses for chimney and sewerage maintenance and other repairs to the mansion during the occupation by the school, which came to approximately £700.

The only problem the school raised was the question of security of tenancy. Since the occupation was merely dependent upon a 'gentleman's agreement', could the school be assured that Longleat would not be requisitioned by any other organization? Would it be preferable to turn the 'gentleman's agreement' into something more legally binding? Lord Bath's lawyers pointed out to their client that as long as the agreement was not formalized, Lord Bath did not have to pay income or surtax, and also His Lordship would not want to 'fetter' his successors (Lord Bath being now in his eightieth year) with a binding commitment after his death. However, the school trustees were assured that Longleat would remain in their hands as long as necessary.

The only moment when this appeared doubtful was in late 1942, when the Army made overtures about requisitioning Longleat. Lord Croft, a friend of Lord Bath, intervened to assure him that only ninety acres were needed for an American hospital in the grounds adjacent to Longleat, and the nearest buildings would be one-hundred yards away from the house. As it turned out, the girls quite enjoyed having the Americans on their doorstep. On one occasion there was a concert, and instead of the genteel classical evening anticipated by staff and pupils, the Americans gave them a foot-stomping jazz session.

Longleat adapted to its role as a school as well as most other stately homes. The drawing room, where many of the treasures were stored, was off-limits except when accompanied by a chaperone. The Great Hall became the school assembly hall. At Christmas, it was used for carol services, at which the 5th Marquess joined the headmistress in reading the lessons. The Red Library was a dining room, and as the students described it, 'lovely old books bound in brown calf all round, portraits of ancestors above, and in the middle – the School tables with china mugs on them'.

The State Dining Room, Saloon and Dress Corridor were dormitories; the Orangery was the art room, and so on. The girls were soon used to sleeping with heavy fringed curtains at their windows, and taking lessons in rooms decorated with richly-embroidered tapestries. Twelve rooms used as dormitories were decorated with Chinese wallpapers dating from 1720–40, executed in China and hung in the early nineteenth century when Wyatville carried out a number of major alterations to the house, depicting people in gardens and surrounded by brilliantly-coloured birds and butterflies. 'The one in Miss Harding's sitting-room is the loveliest, I think,' wrote one young student. 'It is pale blue, and beneath white bamboos are little singing-birds, and tiny Chinese ladies and children sit and play.'

Some of the best furniture was left in the corridors, and girls grew accustomed to Jacobean or William and Mary chairs, and Italian Renaissance chests. They were allowed free access to Longleat's famous libraries, thus learning first-hand some of their country's history. In fact, as the girls soon realized, it was difficult to escape from an overpowering sense of the past. 'I turn into a passage, lined with more ancestral portraits, and it seems as if the flicker of a brocade skirt has just disappeared round the other end, when suddenly a horde of overalled schoolgirls swarms out just behind me, and the illusion is broken.'

The illusion was also broken, of course, by the ever-present reminders of war. School notes in the magazine occasionally refer, in typically laconic style, to the dangers, such as, 'First Air Raid. Four hours spent in cellars.' Or, 'School went to cellars during fourth period as there was an air battle overhead.' 'Two firemen and an instructor came from Warminster to show the Sixth Form, House Prefects and Fire Brigade how to deal with incendiary bombs.' Some of the older girls worked on the local farms, and got involved in other wartime efforts, including, in the summer of 1943, a holiday camp at Longleat with children evacuated from Clapham County Secondary School. 'We all slept in the dormitories with the Chinese wallpaper,' reported two students from the Lower Sixth in the school magazine. 'The Clapham girls did not like this at first. One said, "Oh, I don't like all these funny little people looking at me when I'm in bed," but they soon became used to it.'

The odd mixture of serenity, ancient history and horror inspired by life at Longleat at that time is vividly conveyed in this poignant scene described in the magazine in 1939:

'Sitting in the Great Hall that evening I was aware of talk all around me, but took little part in it. The lights were not on because of the difficulty of "blacking out". The light from the great log fire had a weird way of suddenly picking out an antler here, an embossed figure or carving there, and then dancing off, leaving it in darkness. War seemed impossible, for here it was so warm and peaceful – almost too peaceful to be the home of 250 evacuees. And as I sat on one of our light oak chairs in my school uniform I looked at the coats of arms above me and felt rather small and out of place.'

Perhaps one of the most touching aspects of the Royal School's tenancy was its effect on Lord Bath. Unlike many owners, who either moved out or remained distant from the occupiers, the 5th Marquess took great delight in the girls, and they in him. Boxes of letters he kept and that are housed at Longleat testify to a truly affectionate relationship between them. They sensed his kindness and appreciated his generosity in making over so much of his great house to them. Cards, poems, birthday cakes, wildflowers, were always winging their way to His Lordship's modest ground-floor suite. During an epidemic of mumps, for instance: 'We had a marvellous view of the air fight the other day from the "Mump Room".' And, 'We are swathed in bandages and cotton wool which makes us look like Angora Rabbits.' Another writes after an air raid: 'We went into Sister's Room and lay on the floor with pillows and blankets for three hours. We tried our best to sleep, without much success.' And when Lord Bath's beloved Great Dane, Stephen, died in November 1940, a flood of cards and notes of sympathy arrived at his door. On 12 July 1942, Lord Bath celebrated his eightieth birthday and the girls put on a historical pageant about Longleat and made a birthday cake for him. When they left the school, many wrote to him to thank him for his hospitality or to regret not having said goodbye in person. As one young poet wrote:

> 'In future days when the new word appears,
> Ne'er shall we lose, 'midst all our hopes and fears,
> Enduring love of these our Longleat years.'

Testimony to Lord Bath's pleasure at this late date is a letter he wrote to the school's principal, Miss M. C. Harding: 'I am quite honest that I am enjoying every moment. It is twenty-five years since I had children running about the house; I have enjoyed my life even when alone, but I never realised how lonely I have been, and I love hearing the children all over the place – in fact I keep my door open on purpose.'

While Lord Bath lived in relative seclusion, apart from his young female tenants, there were two visits from Queen Mary to Longleat, and fortnightly ones from the head gardener, who came to cut His Lordship's hair. He had made further retrenchments in his staff, and at his death there was only one indoor servant. The 5th Marquess of Bath died in 1946, and the girls of the Royal School, still in residence, stood in line down the steps of Longleat as his coffin was taken to be buried in Longbridge Deverill.

In 1947, when the school moved out, a school for the children of clergy in Clevedon, Somerset, agreed to buy the property temporarily erected on the Longleat estate by the Royal School for £3,500. Somewhat more than that was needed by the 6th Marquess, back from the war, to pay death duties of £700,000 and to restore Longleat and its 16,000-acre estate to some kind of economic health. He faced a dilapidated house, with much furniture disintegrating in storage; a leaking roof; damaged pictures, fabrics, curtains, tapestries, carpets; and a war-weary estate. The informal agreement with the Royal School remained as unsatisfactory with regard to compensation as the Government's meagre efforts. (Lord Bath's major complaint, however, was lightly aimed at the American residents, whose concrete roads and building foundations were so efficiently laid that removing them cost a small fortune.) His solution, revolutionary at the time but now par for the course, was to open Longleat to the public again as it had been in the early nineteenth century, creating a pleasure-ground that would attract both young and old from all over the country. Today, over half a million visitors a year come to Longleat, and the house and its varied entertainments are one of the major tourist attractions of the world.

The School
BLENHEIM PALACE

*'One would see Classical Scholars studying
Horace in the shadow of the bronze statues in
the water-garden; or naturalists observing the
flora and fauna of the great expanse of
Blenheim Park.'*

–H. C. A. Gaunt, Headmaster,
Malvern College

Blenheim Palace,

WOODSTOCK · OXFORD

NOT EVEN A national monument as precious as Blenheim was immune from the call to war in 1939. The first Duke of Marlborough would no doubt have understood, having won Woodstock Park from Queen Anne as a reward for his military exploits. Tidy minds might have found it appropriate if Marlborough College had taken over Blenheim, but it was Malvern that had the good fortune to find itself transferred there for the first year of the war.

The then-headmaster, H. C. A. Gaunt, tells the story in his brief memoir of the war, *Two Exiles*:

'On Boxing Day, the 26th of December, 1938, among a number of envelopes containing Christmas cards one letter stood out among the rest. It was pale bluish grey, was marked on the outside "Secret and Confidential", and bore the crest of His Majesty's Office of Works on the back of the envelope. Speculating rapidly on what signal honour I was about to be asked to accept, I slit open the envelope. Inside was a second sealed envelope, this time marked "SECRET. To be opened only by H. C. A. Gaunt, Esq., M.A., Headmaster of Malvern College." I complied. It contained a letter from Sir Patrick Duff, Permanent Secretary to the Ministry of Works, informing me that the Government "have had under consideration the question of earmarking a number of large buildings outside London for national purposes in the event of war, and I am afraid it is my ungrateful duty to let you know that Malvern College is one of those earmarked ..."'

Sir Patrick stressed the utmost secrecy of this information, a condition with which the headmaster of Malvern College was happy to comply. Parents were not likely to take quietly to the idea of their boys being moved all over England, nor were prospective parents likely to sign up their boys under such conditions. Only the Chairman and Vice-Chairman of the College were told. However, working in such strict secrecy to find alternative accommodation for some 450 boys was a great hindrance, as well as the discovery that suitable buildings, in particular hotels, demanded very high rents and retainers even if they would consider such a request.

In April 1939, the Headmaster and the Vice-Chairman went back to Sir Patrick Duff, reporting total failure to find somewhere else to house the school. At this point Sir Patrick told them that he had that very morning received a letter from the Duke of Marlborough, offering Blenheim Palace to the Government in case of war. 'But,' Sir Patrick remarked, 'I suppose it would not be large enough for what you want.'

One wonders how big Sir Patrick thought the Palace was. He might also have been reminded of the examples of Stowe and Bryanston, both public schools operating out of former country houses. Blenheim was much bigger than most country houses, and while obviously not equipped to be used as a school, there were certainly enough rooms for boys and staff. Catering facilities seemed adequate too, after the happy event of Lady Sarah Spencer-Churchill's eighteenth birthday, which took place in June 1939. A thousand guests came to a Grand Ball thrown by the Duke, described by one observer as 'perhaps the last great European ball'. The extensive additions to the kitchens installed by the Duke for this occasion were then left for the use of the grateful Malvern staff.

On 1 September 1939, the day of the Polish invasion, representatives of the Office of Works arrived at Malvern College to prepare it for the Admiralty, the military department who had targeted the school buildings. (Winston Churchill was then First Lord of the Admiralty, and there were unsubstantiated rumours that he had expedited Malvern's move to Blenheim.) Gaunt at once began the huge preparations for the exodus, although the requisitioning was still supposed to be secret, and the official requisition order did not arrive until a week later.

On 8 September, the following letter was sent by Headmaster Gaunt to parents:

'I regret to have to tell you that His Majesty's Government have informed me that the Houses and buildings of Malvern College will be required almost immediately for war purposes ... The College will reassemble at Blenheim Palace, Woodstock, the seat of His Grace the Duke of Marlborough. The Palace is large enough to house the entire School and many of the Staff, and the facilities contained in the magnificent buildings and grounds will make it possible for all normal School activities to be continued ... Woodstock itself is in the heart of the country in a reception area, while the Palace itself contains admirable shelter against Air Raids ...

'The continuance of Education is a matter of great national importance, both for the prosecution of the war and for the tasks of reconstruction which will follow when peace returns again. I am entirely confident that with the willing co-operation of all concerned the College in its new surroundings will continue to contribute as greatly towards Public School Education as it has in the past.'

Term was postponed two weeks, and during that time the essentials for school life were transferred to Blenheim Palace. While the first vans started arriving with school equipment, the major question was, what to do about Blenheim's treasures? While the Duke expressed mild concern that the boys might be tempted to use the portraits of his ancestors as dartboards, he was remarkably relaxed about the potential for damage that the school invasion afforded. The lack of available time dictated that while everything easily movable (most of the furniture and antiques) was either evacuated or stored by the Blenheim estate staff, the huge tapestries and paintings would simply have to remain where they are. As much effort as possible was made to protect them. Screens of 'Essex' boarding – all of which had to be installed without the use of nails – were put up around the walls. The yards of priceless parquet flooring were covered with linoleum and coconut matting, 2,400 square yards in all. The beautiful damask curtains were covered in canvas, and pads of felt were affixed to the mahogany doors. Many of the statues were moved into the chapel, which was declared out of bounds to the boys. Those statutes that could not be moved were wrapped in blankets, giving a rather spooky, mummy-like appearance, especially at night, which alarmed the more susceptible younger boys.

Meanwhile, fifty-five vanloads of desks, papers, beds, pianos, tables, and other school paraphernalia arrived at various unorthodox hours, requiring masters to sort and install them as rapidly as possible before the start of term. The State Rooms and Library were converted into dormitories and classrooms, and the Great Hall was designated as the dining room. The old Laundry in the north-east office block became a laboratory, and the riding school an assembly hall and gymnasium.

In spite of the Duke's extensions, two steam ovens, teak sinks, plate racks and shelves had to be installed in the kitchen. New boilers were fitted. Hot water containers were brought in so that food might be transported and served hot in the Great Hall. Sixteen large huts were erected in the main courtyard for extra classrooms and had to be provided with radiators and lamps. This and more details, in Headmaster Gaunt's estimation, came to about £12,000.

In surprisingly short order, the school was functioning normally. As Gaunt wrote, in nostalgic vein: 'Could not Sergeant Major Wilson's fairy voice be heard whispering delicious fooleries under the Palace windows when the O.T.C. squads were at work? Did not Gunster, the School Porter, still dispense small stationery and put up his inimitable notices from his fastness behind a screen in the Great Hall? Could not "Jock" be seen treading the glistening dews of sunny October mornings on the Great Lawn marking out Football Pitches? ... The old things still went on ... Dr Elkington swung his car at the usual speed along the roads of the Park, and with hardly a pause through the narrow archways too! Sister Cherrington, in her beautiful but isolated Sanatorium, tended to the sick as devotedly as ever, though for the whole of her time there she had to work with oil lamps ...'

By 19 October, the headmaster was able to write to parents: 'On Monday we started a full timetable which appears to be running smoothly ... An almost full programme of football has been played this week, and a large number of boys have started work on the Kitchen Garden and the Park Farm, a form of National Service which I believe they are glad to do. Choir and Choral practice is in full swing. Art classes are held and will very soon be normal; the O.T.C. is parading, and the A.R.P. routine is now well-established. Several parents have written to me on this latter point, and I would like to assure you all that quite apart from the fact that the Palace is very unlikely to be deliberately attacked from the air, the basements, with their enormously thick brick walls, provide admirable shelter.'

One of the problems Gaunt did not mention was the behind-the-scenes struggle with the Government over compensation, which seems to have almost driven the headmaster into a psychiatric ward. Displeased as he had been over the summary requisitioning of the school (which he regarded, along with other school headmasters equally displaced, as basically unnecessary), he had to deal with Civil Service stonewalling, both about compensation payments and also about dates for the return of the school to its own buildings.

Nor did Gaunt mention the headaches caused by the laying of a gas line all

A contemporary cartoon gives an amusing picture of the adaptations English country houses had to make after the outbreak of war.

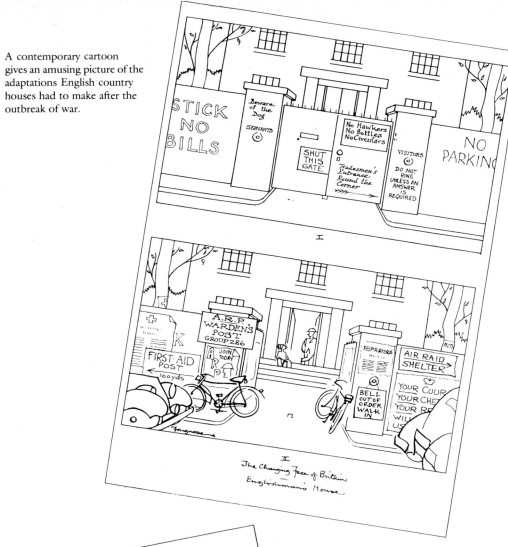

The Changing Face of Britain — Englishman's House

"... I like that! Why, we knew this when it was a pair of park gates!"

Country house-owners spent much of the war attempting to prevent the Ministry of Works from removing the valuable wrought-iron gates and railings from their estates.

It is difficult to believe that the barely distinguishable camouflage draped over Claremont House in Esher, Surrey, could have been effective against German reconnaissance from the air.

A group photograph of the Hawker Aircraft design team outside Claremont House shows the camouflage netting in greater detail.

The dome of Castle Howard goes up in flames in 1940, victim of accident, not of war.

The boys of Malvern School do morning exercises outside Blenheim Palace.

The Great Hall of Blenheim becomes a very imposing school dormitory.

(*Left*) The kitchens at Heath House served admirably for hospital cooks, here helped by two male patients.

(*Below left*) 'The matron, the nurses and the staff, do all they can to make you laugh,' wrote a young bombardier in a poetic tribute to Heath House after convalescing there.

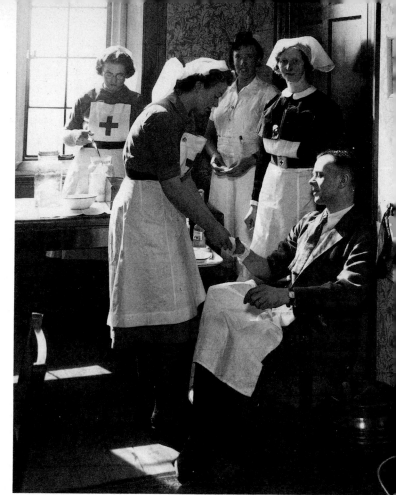

(*Right*) The pantry at Heath House, with a patient whose ship had sunk in the icy waters off north Russia, and whose wounds had frozen during his long ordeal in the sub-zero seas.

(*Below*) The elegant damask wallpaper makes an incongruous background for these two shell-shocked patients at Heath House.

Women were constantly urged to 'do their bit', whether it was riding to hounds or making tea.

The advertising copy for clothing manufacturers stressed comfort and quality for their country-dwelling consumers.

Advertisements of the time made
fun of Hitler as well as evoking the nostalgic
virtues of 18th-century enlightenment.

Life at Lady Harcourt's countr
house, Old Town, combined
working hard looking after the
business of the estate as well a
her family.

Lady Harcourt and her three
children watch the pigs durir
feeding time.

the way from Woodstock to Blenheim to service the kitchen. A team of masters heroically set to work with picks and spades to dig a trench in the Blenheim limestone, until pneumatic drills could get to the scene. The whole operation took four days. 'Even the planting of goalposts meant hours of work with crowbars and pickaxes, so solid is the rock on which Blenheim is built,' recalled a master.

Gaunt kept an equally tactful silence about the difficulties arising from the blackout. Blenheim had at least one thousand windows. Fortunately, many of the rooms had shutters, but not the Great Hall, and the boys had to help hang the blackout curtains each evening by walking along a wide ledge high above the hall – with no protective railing. George Chesterton, a senior, had a fear of heights. 'I did one side and then said please, never again.'

Gaunt also refrained from mentioning the shower arrangements, which were not exactly parent-material. 'Grisly,' was George Chesterton's description. 'They roofed over a stairwell, and constructed showers there which were really pretty primitive and extremely damp, with mushrooms sprouting everywhere. There was also a problem with loos. Of course there were loos in the Palace, but certainly not designed to cater for 400 boys, so they built sixty more back to back round the corner of one of the wings.' Two years earlier, a film on the reign of Queen Victoria had appeared, entitled *Sixty Glorious Years*. The new loos rapidly became known to the boys as the Sixty Glorious Rears.

George Chesterton was seventeen when he went to Blenheim, and like most of his friends, he greatly enjoyed his time there. 'I was just the right age. The facilities for the senior boys were perfect – not nearly so good for the lesser mortals. The first eleven cricket team played on the Great Lawn, on the south front of the Palace, which was an extremely good square and excellent cricket was possible. Within a matter of weeks I threw a cricket ball through one of the Palace windows, which of course had to be one of the original bevelled panes of eighteenth-century glass and impossible to replace. So I was summoned before the Duke, which you can imagine was something of an ordeal. But I think he was more embarrassed than I was, and suggested that I should try not to do it again.'

On happier occasions, prefects and some senior boys were invited sometimes to dinner with the Duke and his family, who retained a wing of the palace and were often at home to the school. An added enticement to this civilized socializing was the presence of the Duke's two daughters, Sarah, just turned eighteen, and her younger sister Caroline, two years younger. Their occasional proximity must have provided delightful compensation for the austerities of public school life.

In spite of the normal school routine, most of the older boys were already thinking in terms of joining up. 'Masters kept disappearing off to the war,' George Chesterton remembers, 'and when the summer term came, with the collapse of France, we all became intensely involved. We had formed a Home Guard. After Dunkirk all our rifles were taken away to give to the Army. Later we were allowed back a skeleton number so we could train in the Park. It was very exciting and we felt we were really part of the war.

'Also being a senior boy I was a member of the palace Fire Brigade. One of our jobs was to patrol the roof at night and watch for incendiary bombs. There were about four acres of roof, and in the dark it was sometimes rather alarming. All this meant, I'm afraid, that academic work came very low on the list for me.'

Fortunately, the patrols proved to be unnecessary, as Blenheim saw no action during that time. One night a warning came that parachutists might drop on country similar to Blenheim's, and for ten days a complete Canadian Armoured Division arrived at Blenheim and filled the Park with guns, anti-aircraft equipment, armoured cars, lorries and tents. During this time, reports Headmaster Gaunt, 'we entertained some 500 men to a great open-air concert on the Palace steps, and a number of boys learned to play Baseball'. The division vanished as suddenly as it had arrived – the kind of mysterious, inexplicable event that took place all over the country during the first years of the war. The only other inconvenience occurred when warning sirens required the boys to remain in the Palace basements well into the night without adequate sleeping arrangements. The next day orders were given for 400 hessian bags to be filled with straw for mattresses, should an emergency like that one happen again. Unfortunately an emergency arose the very next night, before the bags had been finished, and this time the boys had to spend five hours uncomfortably underground, instead of three. 'The First XI played a very weary but very creditable cricket match next day on The Close at Rugby,' reported the proud but no doubt equally weary headmaster.

In an issue of the *Malvernian* published in December 1939, A. H. Dammers (later Dean of Bristol Cathedral) describes some of the effects of the Palace on the students. 'There have been moments of ridiculous sublimity; of watching the intriguing antics of Donald Duck beneath the sightless glare of the swathed, unidentifiable ancestors that hideously grace the lofty grandeur of the long library . . . of turning, like some embryo Archimedes, from the contemplation of Pythagoras to the problem of transferring half a thousand broken plates to the bowels of the Palace by means of a maddeningly temperamental hydraulic lift ... and those quiet half-hours, construing Sophocles astride a leaden sphynx, a dumb creature proud in her impassivity, amid the sunlit plashings and green formality of the lower terrace.'

Sadly for the boys, all this came to an end a year later. The Admiralty decided to relinquish much of Malvern College, retaining only certain buildings for its own use, and so in September 1940 the school was able to return to its proper lodgings. There was a small ceremony of farewell to the Duke and Duchess (and their daughters), and the school equipment was once more loaded on to lorries and taken back to Malvern. (A year later, the school was forced to move again, this time to Harrow. Brave Gaunt. After German intelligence information indicated its safety in Swanage was threatened, the Telecommunications Research Establishment was ordered away from the coast to Malvern, which, owing to its remote location, high hills and proximity to an aerodrome, was a suitable location for one of the country's vital new Radar installations. At least Gaunt had the satisfaction of being able to quote the words of a high official, spoken to him in 1944, that the war against the U-boats and the war in the air had both been won on the Playing Fields of Malvern.)

This was not the end of the war for Blenheim. Shortly after, and under a mantle of intense secrecy, M.I.5 moved in, bringing in something over a thousand workers. (The secrecy was so intense that the conductors of the local bus from Oxford to Woodstock apparently used to call out at the gates of the Palace, 'Anyone for M.I.5?') In the Long Library, the rows of school beds were replaced by a series of little offices with matchboard partitions. David Green, author of *The Churchills of Blenheim*, once asked the Duchess what her father-in-law would have said about these new occupants. 'Nonsense,' she replied. 'We could have never heated the Palace without them. They're keeping the tapestries warm.'

Signs of the army occupation still remain at Blenheim. On the very top floors (called 'Housemaid's Heights') may be seen instructions for military personnel in case of fire and air raid precautions still pinned to the walls, peeling off but untouched for years. The Palace escaped serious damage from bombs, partly it is said because Hitler planned to use Oxford for his headquarters, and therefore the Palace was to be preserved for his personal use. In the event, while military campaigns funded its building, and battles of art, architecture and landscaping helped shape its history, Blenheim survived its most recent war as proudly as the Column of Victory, the first Duke of Marlborough's great monument, standing 134 feet tall in Blenheim's park.

The School
CASTLE HOWARD

*'I remember when the entire length of the
antique passage with all the statues was lined
with chamber pots!'*
– Dame Christian Howard, 1987

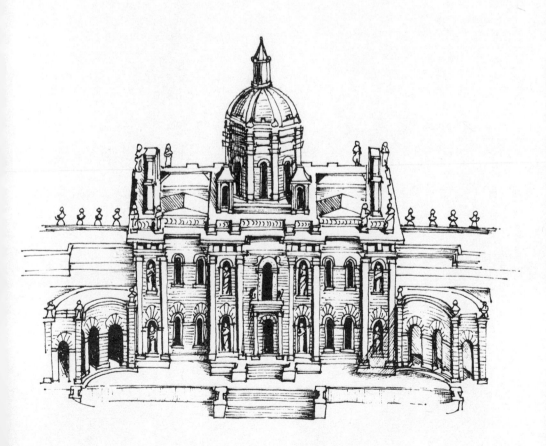

Castle Howard

YORK

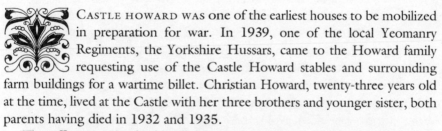CASTLE HOWARD WAS one of the earliest houses to be mobilized in preparation for war. In 1939, one of the local Yeomanry Regiments, the Yorkshire Hussars, came to the Howard family requesting use of the Castle Howard stables and surrounding farm buildings for a wartime billet. Christian Howard, twenty-three years old at the time, lived at the Castle with her three brothers and younger sister, both parents having died in 1932 and 1935.

'The officers ate in the big dining room and used the Canaletti Room as their anteroom,' Dame Christian remembers, 'but when the Army Land Agent arrived and saw the priceless mirrors and furniture everywhere, he hit the roof, imagining a wild night, I suppose. He insisted that they move to less pretentious quarters, so the Officers' Mess went into what we called the basement, although it wasn't really since it is at ground level.

'Then the medical officers arrived and were horrified at the conditions the men were living in. The officers were all right, having been allowed to stay in the Castle, but most of the men were living in granaries and so on. I believe their horses had all been brought over from Poland to be trained on manoeuvres, and the officers seemed to have been mainly concerned to find good stabling for the horses.

'So these troops moved out, and instead we got the Territorial Battalion of the West Yorkshire Regiment. Before the war started, the size of the Territorial Army had been doubled in preparation for hostilities. The trouble was that while some regiments had a lot of prestige, this one was perhaps not so attractive, and its Territorial Battalion being short of volunteers had been augmented by Militiamen, who were the first conscripts. We had a very nice Captain in charge, but no one could have said he was the world's best organizer or disciplinarian, so it was a little difficult. Much the best value was the padre. I am still in touch with him.'

In the first winter of the war, the authorities of Queen Margaret's School in Scarborough began to get very nervous. The school had been badly bombarded in World War One, and whenever the wireless announced that the Germans were bombing the north-east coast the parents assumed it was Scarborough. The governing body of Queen Margaret's, the Woodard Society (northern chapter), had already approached the Trustees of Castle Howard about a possible option to rent the Castle for another of the Society's schools. However, under increasing pressure from Queen Margaret's, in January 1940 the Society and the Trustees agreed that the Scarborough school would move in for a term from 6 April 1940, until the cessation of hostilities between the UK and Germany. When this agreement was completed, the Army agreed to give up its billets, and the school moved in at Easter 1940.

'There was quite a lot of hassle with the Army moving out and the school moving in. The Army had suddenly received orders to go to Norway. In the end they went to Iceland, poor dears. So everything was a bit of a shambles, and everybody's nerves were jangled. I remember I was in the upstairs nursery/pantry one day in the middle of all this when I heard a crack and a window broke. Quite clearly some wretched soldier had let off his gun and smashed the window.

'When the school arrived, we moved out of the house altogether into the Gate House. This had originally been built, probably as an Inn, on either side of an earlier Vanbrugh Gateway. By 1940 it consisted of a farmhouse on the west side (rebuilt in 1928 after a fire) and the original eastern end into which we moved. Of course it took time to get it ready, so I went back to London, where I was a theological student, after the school had moved in and Nanny supervised our installation into the Gate House. My eldest brother, Mark, was an officer in the Coldstream Guards, my second brother, George, was just beginning his army training (he was later an officer in the Green Howards, our local regiment, and then attached to the Indian Army), my third brother,

Christopher, left Eton that summer to go into the Air Force, and my nine-year-old sister had a governess.

'Most of the furniture was moved and stored in the basement, apart from what we took to the Gate House. We also took some of the pictures, but the rest were left where they were. We took the best pair of mirrors. The others were screwed to the walls, mostly in the Long Dining Room. The Brussels Tapestries were left in the Tapestry Room (used as a Sixth Form Room).'

By April 1940, about 100 girls and teachers were safely installed at their new home. Anne Warin (*née* Hollis) remembers that first idyllic summer there. 'It seemed an Arcadian existence to wander in those classically laid out grounds, to sit and study on the sunny slopes of the temples or beside the lake, and to live in those magnificent rooms. But as time went on there was a tension between this idyll and what was happening in the real world outside. We could hear the throb and drone of our bombers going out on their nightly missions, and especially disturbing were the golden summer days of Dunkirk.' For this reason Anne Hollis left school a year early to join the WRNS. 'There were rebellious teenagers even then!'

In November of that 'idyllic' year, a fire broke out that, while not attributable to the war, badly damaged Vanbrugh's great architectural masterpiece and had repercussions that lasted until long after the war was over.

'While some speak of the school as having "burnt Castle Howard", this is unjust,' declares Dame Christian Howard. 'What happened will always be a little unclear, but I think the best explanation is this. The Army had been in the so-called basement. They had the Colonnade for the officers' mess, and next door they had an anteroom, which had once been a housekeeper's room, for a sitting room. Now you must imagine right through that cold winter of 1939–40, roaring fires going all the time – probably wood and coal – in those rooms, leaving a tough and resinous soot. Then the Army left, and the housekeeper's room was assigned to the senior music mistress, who had her piano in it and taught in it. So certainly there continued to be fires there every day, and I'm pretty sure that it was there that the fire started. Afterwards, we had a fire expert check all the chimneys and six were found in a dangerous condition. We had had a fire eight years earlier in 1932, and we thought that was an electrical fire, but nobody knew for sure.

'I think it was the Secretary in the room above the little dining room who first discovered it, very early on the morning of 9 November 1940. She saw more or less a whole wall on fire. Members of the staff were alerted, and they telephoned to the estate men in the village to ask them to send for the local Malton Fire Brigade. But these men did not realize the school expected them to do the summoning, and meanwhile the school's telephone was cut by the fire. At about half-past-six I heard the pealing of the bell at the Gate House, and I rushed down and there was the senior physical education teacher who had run to us to say, "The house is on fire, can you ring the York Fire Brigade?" I could see the flames but did not know how bad it was. I rang the York Fire Brigade who said, understandably, that they could only be called in by the Malton Fire Brigade. So there was this terrible delay, for Malton had not received any call, and it was two hours before we realized this and finally got them to come.

'My brother Christopher was staying, so he and I went down to the house, while my sister remained with the governess. My Nanny came too with all the keys of our storerooms so she could get at everything. I had three different lots of boots on that day.'

When they arrived at the burning building, the school staff and girls were already in the midst of a desperate effort to save Castle Howard's treasures. The younger girls had been sent to the air raid shelters in the basements, while the older girls were conscripted to help rescue pictures and other valuables. Anne Warin, a Sixth Former at the time, points out the irony that while the school, fearing Air Raids, held frequent Air Raid practices, they rarely if ever had Fire Drill. Mrs Warin has written an account of the fire, and describes the task they faced:

'We went through two form rooms until we reached V.A., the Reynolds Room, and here we found three staff tugging at the pictures. The pictures in this room were immense portraits, one of which took up nearly a whole wall. There was not time to unscrew the rails on which they were hung, and the ladders that we had were not nearly long enough to enable us to reach their tops, so we just had to tug at them until the wires broke and they crashed on top of us. We then took them into the Long Gallery, which was at that time a safe distance from the fire. Many of the pictures crashed from their frames when they fell, and the bare canvases were taken along to the Gallery. Somebody suggested getting into the studio and trying to rescue the priceless mirrors which hung there. On opening the door, however, we discovered that the fire had already claimed them, for it had reached the studio, and the windows and mirrors were cracked and falling in, while flames licked up the walls.'

The girls meanwhile hastily got dressed in clothes fetched by the staff from the dormitories – all different sizes and shapes thrown gratefully on dirty, tired young bodies. 'We tried to rescue the tapestries from the Tapestry Room, but we could only reach one.' The rest were, however, eventually saved by the estate men, who cut them down.

'. . . It was by this time about seven o'clock, and the fire was at its height, when an air raid warning came through, and it was the only time in the whole day when the staff began to look desperate, for they all suspected that, drawn by the glow (which must have been seen for miles and miles), enemy planes would be returning to bomb what they supposed they had set on fire.'

Fortunately, the Germans failed to score, and the rescue work continued. For Christian Howard, it must have been the most painful case of *déjà vu*. 'I had been there eight years ago, and I knew the difference. The fire had a hold on so much of the house this time. When the flames had got into the High Saloon (or were likely to), our chauffeur smashed the windows to try to get the water to it. Then I saw what was happening to the dome. A spark from the fire, which was ablaze on the whole of the eastern part of the South Front, flew off and landed on the very top of the lantern and we saw it gradually burn down.'

With the destruction of the dome, the fire seemed gradually to abate. The York Fire Brigade had also arrived by that time, and was on top of the roof of the Vanbrugh central block, pouring water down through the roof. The garden was full of things that had been rescued from the house, including bedding, clothes, carpets, books, pictures – and crosses and vases from the chapel.

'The next day, when I went to see the damage, the Hall was rubble,' Dame Christian says, 'and all the lead from the roof had melted so that it poured onto the floor. But the most amazing sight was the pile of twenty-foot-long and one-foot-thick oak beams that had held up the dome, in charred ruins. One of the beams had hit a statue above the fireplace and had taken two stone steps from out of the staircase behind as it fell. The floor was damaged here and there but has never been relaid. The most remarkable thing is that the glass in the north front door never broke.'

During the next few days, parents came to fetch the girls and the Howards returned to the Gate House. They also took in three girls from the school, daughters of Bishop Kirk of Oxford, who was unable to fetch them home.

In the months that followed, Christian Howard had to make endless lists for insurance purposes, although 'we were all suffering from shock'. (The inventory made on the entry of the school was woefully inadequate.) All the mirrors in the Long Dining Room and the Chinese Chippendale ones in the Garden Hall were gone, as well as the paintings in the little sitting room and dining room. Some Canalettos were saved, and the tapestries. Perhaps the most poignant loss was that noted by Anne Warin in her memoir: 'Mrs Golding, the senior music mistress, lost her whole home, for her room at Castle Howard was the only home she had, and her most precious possessions, including a beautiful grand piano, were destroyed.'

Meanwhile, in one of the superhuman efforts that seem to exemplify the restoration programmes embarked on during the war, Castle Howard was dried out, cleaned up, and given a temporary roof where the dome had been, just before the snow came. 'There were problems in getting the house ready for the school to return to (in late January or early February, at the same time as dealing with insurance claims, which meant where possible NOT moving damaged furniture, while of course the school wanted them moved to get rooms ready!). Then there were lists of lost and damaged pictures and their frames to be drawn up. Most of our furniture had been stored in the basement and much was soaked from the fire hoses. This furniture, when dried out, went for storage to Bransdale Lodge in the Yorkshire Moors.

'But one day Nanny came to me and said "Christian, we've got to have somewhere in the house to keep some of our things, they can't all stay in the Gate House." So I went to the school authorities to negotiate some space – rooms they certainly weren't going to use, really dungeon-like rooms. But the bursar demurred. However, he played into my hands. They wanted us to move all the statues in one of the corridors because the senior school was going to have a north-facing passage as their dining room. That was fine, but there was the question of moving Ceres, who was a very solid statue indeed, standing on a heavy stone plinth. In order to move her, the builders would have to cut away bits of the plinth and heave it up, which could only be done with the permission of my Trustees. So I said to the bursar, "I believe you do not have permission to move Ceres. However, if you allow me to have these modest rooms, I might be able to help you out . . ." Game, set and match to us!'

Another story involving statuary comes from Anne Warin, who recalls that in one of the passageways leading to the classrooms stood the vast nude sculpture of The Dying Gaul, which, like Ceres, was too big to move, and also too big (or perhaps too recalcitrant) to be censored by a fig leaf. The challenge was a novel one for the 200 or so schoolgirls. 'We all walked past it with averted eyes.'

While the Castle Howard interiors were being scrutinized by the school, the Park had not escaped notice. Like most sizeable country house estates, at the outbreak of war it had been earmarked by the War Agricultural Executive for ploughing up, and its subsequent history is typical of how such land fared under requisitioning.

'Until the war, the Park was rough grazing with a good deal of bracken,' explains Christian Howard. 'The War Agricultural Executive served notice on the farm tenant that he must plough up a certain amount. He had of course no implements or facilities for such large-scale arable farming, so the War Ag. said they would take over half the farm and plough it up themselves. The tenant said he could not make a living on the remainder so they took the whole lot over and he had to move to another small farm on the estate.

'The War Ag. fenced in much of the land in order to keep out the herd of fallow deer but the deer jumped everything so they were slaughtered. (I believe they promised to restore them after the war but nothing came of that.) Recent improved farming methods enabled the bracken to be killed and so most of the land was put under wheat and other cereal crops. Because of the desperate need for the grain, the traditional rotation of crops was abandoned and as a result, the crops got smaller each year. In theory, the land should have been fertilized to prevent this. When George took back the farm after the war, a Land Tribunal made the War Ag. pay compensation for the fertility they had taken out of the land and not replaced!'

While the Castle and the Park played their wartime roles, Dame Christian continued studying theology and then teaching at Chichester High School from 1943 to 1945, spending the holidays at the Gate House and keeping an eye on the Castle. Sadly, Mark and Christopher were both killed in action in July and October 1944.

The school remained at Castle Howard until the end of the war, and then stayed on afterwards, having entered into negotiations to buy the house. The school buildings in Scarborough had been completely destroyed by enemy action – the decision to move to Castle Howard being an example of an evacuation that saved hundreds of lives. The Woodard Society continued to press the family to sell, but negotiations were halted until George, the only remaining heir, returned from the war in August 1945. The Trustees had been at one time convinced the family would never again live at Castle Howard, but George and his wife Cecilia had other ideas. The school finally left in 1951 and two years later the family moved back in. 'Everyone thought we were mad. We had to sue the school for dilapidations, which they had agreed to pay in our lease but disputed the amount. It certainly wasn't easy. But Castle Howard is a house with a very strong feeling. It was a very happy house. When the school moved in, there was an absence of feeling. But when the family moved in again the happiness came back.'

It is thought that the insurers paid out the whole sum for which the house was covered but of course, by the time restoration could begin, that did not cover all that had to be done. Much work was started in the 1950s, including the rebuilding of the dome, and the recreation of its Pellegrini ceiling, painted by Scott Medd. The outside restoration followed Vanbrugh's original design, but, in the last decade, the Garden Hall and Canaletti Room have been restored to new designs. George Howard (created Lord Howard of Henderskelfe in 1983) died in 1984 and the house passed to his sons: the third son, Simon, and his wife now live in this 'happy house'. Today Castle Howard, having survived two fires and two World Wars, remains not only one of the architectural wonders of northern England, but is probably imprinted on the minds of millions of people as the archetypal English country house, thanks to its major role in the televised version of *Brideshead Revisited*.

The School
KNEBWORTH HOUSE

'When war clouds gathered overhead
And evacuees to the country fled,
The Lytton arms were opened wide,
Offering us a place to hide.'

– Froebel student, 1984

Knebworth House

KNEBWORTH · HERTFORDSHIRE

THIS ANCIENT HOUSE was given a high Gothic façade by the Victorian politician and novelist, Edward Bulwer-Lytton, whose extravagant romantic taste also influenced the interior decoration. His colourful style was passed on to his son, the first Earl of Lytton, Viceroy of India, also a literary figure and poet. Thus the 2nd Earl of Lytton and his beautiful wife, the former Pamela Plowden, entered the war as heirs to a house steeped in literary and poetic tradition. Lord Lytton cut a romantic figure himself, as James Lees-Milne, visiting Knebworth in 1942, describes in his diary: 'He is tall, immaculately dressed in a black suit with a long, thin gold chain round his neck, the end of the chain hidden in a waistcoat pocket. He has silvery hair, curling at the back . . .' Lees-Milne preferred His Lordship's looks to those of Knebworth House, which he called 'undeniably hideous'. Whatever its external appearance, Knebworth's spacious rooms and large parkland were an obvious target for requisitioning once war broke out. They fell to the Froebel Institute, a training college for teachers, which moved into the house from Roehampton in October 1939.

It is not recorded how Froebel and the Lytton family got together, but Lord Lytton did not make the agreement without careful consideration of every option available to him. In May 1939 his estate manager, H. Cartwright, drew up a comparison of financial advantages and disadvantages of Lord Lytton living at Knebworth House himself during a war, or of letting it to the Froebel Institute while living at the Manor House or other house of equivalent value. According to Cartwright's estimates, Lord Lytton would save roughly 400 pounds a year by moving out of Knebworth and living at the Manor House (he would pay much less in rates and gardeners' wages, for instance). Cartwright also pointed out that if Lord Lytton went on living at Knebworth, he would no doubt have to have evacuees. 'There are roughly fifty habitable rooms but if thirty evacuees lived there at five shillings a week they would provide an income of £390 a year. Wear and tear would however be very heavy.' At this time, besides the Froebel discussions, there was some possibility that the Sun Insurance Company might want Knebworth, which Cartwright thought would be the best solution, since the insurance company would pay a far higher rent than that suggested by Froebel.

In the end, Froebel won the day, and in July 1939, negotiations were completed. The lease seems to have included only a token rent, as Cartwright had feared (rates for the first year came to only twelve shillings). With it came an understanding that during their occupation, the Froebel people were liable for any expenditure normally undertaken by Lord Lytton. If, however, any of that expenditure accrued to Lord Lytton's benefit, such portion would be refunded. Otherwise, the house was to be returned to the owner in the same condition as it had been in at the start of the occupation. Lord and Lady Lytton were to move out to the Manor House, along with the best furniture, small *objets d'art*, and some favourite books, which included two volumes of Browning.

Knebworth was already well prepared for war. Air Raid Precautions had been in effect since 1938. Elaborate A R P exercises were performed under the guidance of 'umpire' Cartwright, with pretend incendiary bombs falling on the house and other dramas created with evident gusto. 'A housemaid is seen calling for help from the battlement on the roof over the State Drawing Room,' read the operation orders for 9 and 10 August 1939. 'She is trapped by the flames and is unable to reach another part of the roof. (The housemaid will be represented by a dummy for the purposes of this incident.)' Blackout fabric had been ordered from Hitchin. Local people had been permitted by Lord Lytton to practise driving without lights in Knebworth Park, with the proviso that they not drive too close to the lake grounds.

So when Froebel moved in, much was already in place. But as with so many institutional occupations of large old country houses, a major problem arose immediately. The waterworks that had been perfectly adequate for Lord and

Lady Lytton totally collapsed when required to cope with 100 students. Miss Eglantine Jebb, the formidable principal of the Froebel Institute, spent much of those early months extending the drainage system, while assuring the estate office that this was the responsibility of the college. Other small details were quickly taken care of, such as two plaster figures in the hall that fell down 'of their own accord'. Lord Lytton agreed to have them taken away and stored. Mr Cattell, replacing Mr Cartwright who had gone to the war, noticed that the girls from the school were cycling around the Park across the grass between the top of the lime avenue by the corner of the Church to Buckhorn Lodge. 'I shall be grateful if you will give instructions for the practice to be stopped.' There was rat trouble. The roof leaked. The cellars, being used as Air Raid Shelters for the girls, needed new exits. Partitions were needed in the hall – but must be installed without nails or screws. Who was responsible for mowing? For path maintenance?

Letters flew between Miss Jebb and Mr Cattell. 'Dear Miss Jebb, can you possibly tell me where you have put the Chinese lantern which hung in the hall at the foot of the oak staircase?' 'Dear Mr Cattell, I have to report to you that a further piece of stained glass fell from the Armoury on Friday night, and another pane with the leading looks as if it might fall shortly ...' (This was the result of a bomb that fell on Lytton Lodge in November 1940, also damaging the window of Mrs Bulwer Lytton's bedroom at the house.) Tempers grew short. 'Although every effort is made to fulfil your requirements as soon as possible, you must realize the difficulties which beset us in obtaining the same service from those we employ as in pre-war days ...' 'May I draw your attention to my letter of 13 February in which I asked you to be so good as to let me know the estimated cost *before* instructions were issued to proceed ...' 'Would you kindly let me know who was instructed by Lord Lytton to put down the cement over the floor in the front hall in order to level it, as some of this has broken away, and I shall have to get it repaired as it is rather dangerous? ...'

These disputes over liability were the inevitable result of two opposing groups protecting their interests, and dogged almost everybody involved in the occupation of other people's houses. While the day-to-day negotiations continued backstage, so to speak, the general relationship between Lord Lytton and the school was extremely friendly. Lord Lytton himself became very fond of Miss Jebb and enjoyed giving talks and readings to the students. A poem written many years later by one of those present describes the scene:

'Lord Lytton sometimes came along
To watch us act and hear our songs.
Now and then he would recite
His father's poems, to our delight.
The acoustics in this splendid Hall
Carried his faultless voice to all.'

They were young teachers in training, not schoolgirls, to the great dis-
appointment of the Headmistress of Clifton Grange, a neighbouring school.
On discovering Knebworth had been taken over, she wrote to the authorities
with great enthusiasm: 'Would you kindly let me know the name of the school
which is in residence at the moment at Knebworth, as if it is a girls' school
we might be able to arrange Matches?'

While forgoing the pleasure of matches against Clifton Grange, the young
women found much to enjoy at Knebworth. 'I am proud to have had the
fortune to have slept in Queen Elizabeth's Bed, for all the nine months I was
there,' recalls Theodosia Lopez. 'The room contained three or four other
beds, so what with chests of drawers, etc., the panelling round the room was
practically invisible. We named the two figures holding up the "roof" of the
bed Nervo and Knox, who were two (rather vulgar) comedians of that time.'
Although the students were at least seventeen years old, there were obvious
precautions – no smoking, except in one area behind the kitchens, no food in
rooms. Miss Jebb forbade the use of ink in the picture gallery. Only the staff
were permitted to use the State Rooms behind the Banqueting Hall (where
the students had their meals). Mrs Lopez remembers a few servants in the
house, but the girls had to take turns to do some housework. 'I remember
dusting the bannisters of the Minstrels' Gallery rather sketchily.' She also
remembers an incredible loo. 'One mounted two steps to sit on a flower-
painted pedestal, and instead of pulling a chain one lifted a lever. It was called
St John's because it was by St John's Bedroom, now in the private part of the
house.'

During this time, Lord Lytton was deeply worried about the future of
Knebworth. His eldest son, Lord Knebworth, had been killed in a flying
accident in 1933, and his second son was fighting in Africa. According to
James Lees-Milne, who went round Knebworth with him in June 1942, Lord
Lytton was determined to return to the house after the war. He had worked
on restoration of the house with Sir Edwin Lutyens, who was his brother-in-
law, and believed that offering it, and the 3,000 acre estate, to the National
Trust, would be the best guarantee of its survival. Lees-Milne describes the

state of the interior of Knebworth then as 'shoddy'. 'The only room that I liked was the Palladianized great hall. Lord Lytton has had the paint stripped off the wainscote. He said it was the first stripping to be undertaken in England.' Lees-Milne adds, 'At present the Froebel Girls' College is installed in the house, which becomes them.'

A month after this visit, the new Lord Knebworth was killed in Libya. His sister, Lady Hermione Cobbold, inherited his share of the estate, and after some frank speaking with Lees-Milne, the National Trust discussions were dropped. Lord Lytton, now with both his sons dead, had to go on grappling with Knebworth alone.

The Froebel Institute gave its official evacuation notice for the end of August 1945. There were tentative talks about the college continuing to rent the house, but difficulties in finding domestic staff, because of both the house's isolated position and its lack of modern equipment, rendered it an impractical proposition. In March 1946, Froebel paid Knebworth House £1,950 in dilapidations. A small dispute over the settlement involved garden produce and fruit, which was not paid for by Froebel at the beginning of the tenancy on the understanding that Lord Lytton would be left an equivalent amount. At the termination of the occupation, the estimable Mr Cattell claimed the sum of £50 for deficiencies of fruit and garden produce. Lord Lytton himself was to be the arbiter of this dispute. His judgement was not recorded.

Mr Cattell also drew up for Lord Lytton some figures about his prospects for Knebworth House after the war. In November 1945, he estimated that the cost to Lord Lytton of living at Knebworth House would be £4,288. 6. 0, per year. Of maintaining the house unoccupied but furnished, £2,633.17. The estimated cost to Lord Lytton of remaining at the Manor House, £2007. 16. 9. The estimated saving if Knebworth House were let at £1,500 per year would be over £2,000.

As it turned out, the issue became academic. In 1946, Lord Lytton sold a collection of Period, Italian and French furniture and *objets d'art*. In 1947 he died. The house passed down to his daughter, Lady Hermione Cobbold, and the Cobbold family lives there still.

The Military Billet
GREAT GLEMHAM
HOUSE

'We never thought we'd go back . . .'
– The Dowager Countess of Cranbrook, 1987

Great Glemham House

SAXMUNDHAM · SUFFOLK

GREAT GLEMHAM HOUSE is a large family house dating from 1814, situated in a corner of rural Suffolk, close (significantly close as it turned out) to the East Anglia coast, the vulnerable hump north of Harwich, not far from Aldeburgh, where Benjamin Britten lived and worked. This part of Suffolk was also the inspiration for George Crabbe, the Aldeburgh-born poet who provided some of Britten's operatic ideas. E. M. Forster wrote, 'To talk about Crabbe is to talk about England.' To talk about this corner of Suffolk during the Second World War is also to talk about England, at a moment in her history when poetry and music seemed like distant dreams.

The big house had not been long owned by its current residents. The 3rd Earl of Cranbrook, a sick man, bought it in 1914, after moving to Suffolk for its supposedly healthy climate. He died soon after. When the Second World War broke out, the Cranbrooks were in their summer cottage in Westmorland. Jock, the 4th Earl, immediately returned to Glemham, leaving behind three children and his wife, Fidelity, pregnant with their fourth. Lord Cranbrook immediately moved all the best furniture, china and paintings into the drawing room, and locked it up. The house was then made ready for its first wartime occupants – children from nursery schools in Leytonstone, outside London.

Between 1939 and 1940, the school was in residence. But in the late spring of 1940, when the German invasion was expected any minute – the first wave, obviously, on the East Coast – the school was closed and the Army took its place. By this time Lady Cranbrook and her family were living close by at the White House farm, while her husband took up his duties in Cambridge as deputy regional commissioner, Eastern Region, from Cambridge to the Wash.

'The point about the house was that it was a transit place for Yorkshire, Lancashire and Scottish regiments, which meant that nobody took much care about it,' recalls the Dowager Countess of Cranbrook. 'The Colonel and the officers were billeted in Little Glemham, about three miles away; the sergeants and enlisted men were at the big house. The back part of the house was used for officers of the Home Guard, and also for our old servant, James, to keep an eye on things.'

James had his work cut out. One merry night the soldiers turned on all the bidets and bathtubs upstairs and everything flooded. The water seeped into a cornice over the drawing room, and water remained in this cornice throughout the war, so the whole of one wall suffered wet rot. 'James was always discovering soldiers trying the lock into the drawing room,' says Lady Cranbrook, 'but I used to do much more basic things like prowl around the back of the house. One lot I remember used to sweep up all the dirt, food, scraps and so on into heaps all the way down the back passage, smelling horrible and of course enticing rats and mice. I used to spend my time going round to the officers' mess or ringing up complaining bitterly. "Oh, surely not, Lady Cranbrook," they'd say. "Well, for God's sake come and look!" I'd cry.'

The men sometimes tried to be helpful. 'I remember one terrible day when I went over there, one of the officers invited me in and said, "We'd like to show you something. We've redecorated your dining room for you." And they had. They'd painted the dining room an institutional, shiny, strong green up to dado height, and then brown. And they'd done it all over the stonework, the fireplace, the mantelpiece, everything. I gave a sort of gasp as he said, "Don't you think it looks nice and clean?"'

Meanwhile the Cranbrooks were in a small farmhouse, looking after six children, including cousins, listening for bombs, keeping the blackout, and enjoying unexpected benefits such as a good supply of fresh vegetables from the local garden. The children kept an eye on the big house too. 'They used to say things like, "I hope they haven't taken our toys." And they were furious when the soldiers cut down their swings.' But the chief danger in their vulnerable coastal position was from German snipers, who used to fly close to the ground and shoot at anything they fancied. 'I remember one coming round in the fog (they always chose misty days, of course) at Christmastime in 1941. It shot a few holes in the lead roof of the big house, causing still more damage, came down the field, shot at a cart and horse which bolted, flew right past my window while the children rushed in screaming, and then went back home.'

The children enjoyed most of this, bicycling to examine bomb craters and collect souvenirs. But there were some uncomfortable moments for their mother. 'We had a little school in the village, and the children had to walk through the park of the big house to get to the village and so to school. One day, they came back saying, "There's a very funny man by a post we saw when we were going to school. When we came back he was still there." It was one of the soldiers. A suicide. He had hung himself on a post in the park.'

In 1943 the Americans came to operate the aerodrome only half a mile from Great Glemham House. For strategic reasons there was an air base every five miles along that coastal part of Suffolk. They made a lot of noise. There were battle areas, where the military did manoeuvres. But as in most parts of Britain, life and work went on. 'We had some German prisoners of war to help with the sugar-beet harvest,' recalls Lady Cranbrook. 'Our old foreman, Cobbin, used to look them up and down very carefully to see if any of them looked like their fathers. I don't know what he was going to do if he recognized any – kill them, I suppose!'

Village activities continued also. Americans were very popular with the local girls. 'They were much better-looking and they had much nicer uniforms and lots of money.' But the most memorable scandal involved not a GI but a Scottish deserter. 'He sneaked out of the big house and popped into bed with a certain young woman, and was not discovered until after his unit had left. Her husband returned ten months later and found he had Scottish twins! I suppose people in the village knew, but no one said a word . . .'

In 1945 it was all over and the Cranbrooks were left, as so many families were, to pick up the pieces. Great Glemham House was a sorry sight. Some bannisters were ripped away. The wet rot had seeped into the drawing room treasures. The floors were wrecked. The roof leaked. At the end of the war the Cranbrooks had been cultivating a market garden, and the seeds for the nursery were all spread out in the big house bedrooms. 'We never thought we'd go back.'

Of course not. They had learned to live in a small space, with no proper help. To move back was a formidable thought. 'Before the war we'd had five maids and a nanny, and now we had a daily and someone who came in to cook a midday meal. A lot of houses were pulled down for less. You can see why.'

But the Cranbrooks, with their growing family of five, finally decided to rehabilitate Great Glemham House. 'We simply made the big house smaller. We turned some of the space into flats, and made a kitchen in the old pantry nearer the centre of the house. We sanded the floors. We painted everything and it crumbled at once because you could not get proper paint. But we discovered it was perfectly possible to live without all that staff.'

There were other tiny compensations, besides the financial compensation they were able to claim from the Government, which helped. The last lot of occupants had been the Signals Corps. Outside their Nissen huts in the park, many of these soldiers had made little gardens. 'Even when the huts came down,' Lady Cranbrook remembers fondly, 'the gardens remained.'

As was the case with many country houses, in 1939–45 the park at Glemham was ploughed up for the first time in its history. The ploughed-up parkland revealed the remains of the foundations of a house. It turned out that this was one of the houses where George Crabbe had lived, a house that until that moment had never been located. So in spite of six years of hardship and loss, Great Glemham House finally recovered its children, and Suffolk its most famous poet.

The Military Billet
HAZELLS HALL

*'I'm not quite sure what compulsory powers the
Air Ministry has, but I believe they are pretty
extensive.'*

– Leslie Pym, MP, 1936

Hazells Hall

SANDY · BEDFORDSHIRE

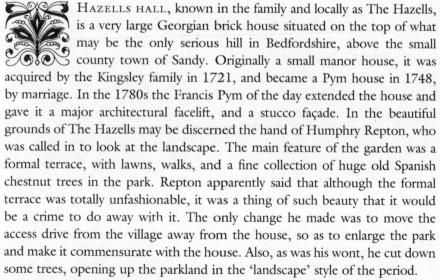 HAZELLS HALL, known in the family and locally as The Hazells, is a very large Georgian brick house situated on the top of what may be the only serious hill in Bedfordshire, above the small county town of Sandy. Originally a small manor house, it was acquired by the Kingsley family in 1721, and became a Pym house in 1748, by marriage. In the 1780s the Francis Pym of the day extended the house and gave it a major architectural facelift, and a stucco façade. In the beautiful grounds of The Hazells may be discerned the hand of Humphry Repton, who was called in to look at the landscape. The main feature of the garden was a formal terrace, with lawns, walks, and a fine collection of huge old Spanish chestnut trees in the park. Repton apparently said that although the formal terrace was totally unfashionable, it was a thing of such beauty that it would be a crime to do away with it. The only change he made was to move the access drive from the village away from the house, so as to enlarge the park and make it commensurate with the house. Also, as was his wont, he cut down some trees, opening up the parkland in the 'landscape' style of the period.

The Pyms lived there happily until 1860, when the head of the family was killed in a train accident at Hatfield – the first fatal accident of the Great Northern Railway, of which the Francis Pym of the day was a director. His

111

son inherited the house, and in 1900 stripped it of its stucco, revealing the red brick that can be seen today. He died in 1927 without heirs, so his brother Frederick, also a bachelor, inherited the mansion, and was living there with a butler and small staff when war broke out in 1939.

As early as 1936 the area around Sandy had been pinpointed as a strategic site for the country's defence in the case of war. A form letter to Mr Pym from the Commandant of the Observer Corps in Uxbridge, Kent, dated 5 March 1936, explained to the old gentleman that 'a system of observer posts manned when necessary by local Special Constables, forms an important part of the arrangements for the Air Defence of Great Britain. By this means, information would be given to Headquarters, Air Defence of Great Britain, as to the movements of any hostile aircraft entering these shores.' The letter went on to state that it was desired to establish such a post at Sandy. No rent was to be paid.

Also in 1936 there were definite intimations of plans to build an aerodrome in the area. The land agent, Mr Preedy, was naturally worried about this possibility, since an aerodrome would require about 400 acres, thus ruining the landscape, the shooting rights, and much of the market gardening land round Everton. Leslie Pym, Member of Parliament for Monmouthshire, Fred's cousin and heir to The Hazells, stepped in at this point, noting to Mr Preedy, 'I'm not quite sure what compulsory powers the Air Ministry has, but I believe they are pretty extensive.' Mr Pym was worried about the question of compensation for such a project. 'Will you let me know any further details you may gather,' he added, 'as I have one or two friends at the Air Ministry?' Evidently. Shortly after, the proposal was abandoned.

By 1940, The Hazells was being examined for potential requisitioning by both the Army and the Red Cross. It was an eminently suitable prospect. The house was exceedingly large, and unoccupied except for Fred Pym, then in his late seventies, who used a few downstairs rooms, plus bedrooms for guests who came frequently to stay. The great drawing room was not used except for storage of furniture at one end, nor was the dining room, and most of the back part of the house was empty.

It was earmarked by the 117th Field Regiment of the 2nd London Division for possible troop accommodation, and was formally requisitioned in January 1941, with the usual compensation clauses. Already a large quantity of ammunition was stored in small sheds scattered throughout the woodlands of the estate. The Army finally decided to use The Hazells as a tactical school for officers and by the end of 1941 the 2nd Corps Junior Leaders' School had moved into the house. 'This presented no problem to my cousin Fred,' recalls

Lord Pym. 'They let him stay in the few rooms he had been living in and were very nice to him.' Some of the furniture was removed to storage in one of the farm buildings, including three stuffed animals' heads, a pair of racing pictures by Ben Herring, a circular birch commode, an old oak cigar cupboard, three pairs of brass candlesticks, five volumes of Macaulay's history and two volumes of *Burke's Landed Gentry*. The school rented the rest of The Hazells' furniture for the modest sum of twenty-six shillings a week (the most expensive items being the dining room furniture, which cost six shillings and threepence a week). A Captain Turner gave Fred Pym a handwritten note, guaranteeing to 'look after all furniture left in rooms used by officers and will compensate for any damage done'.

The usual problems associated with military occupation arose, including the continual encroachment on the surrounding land by army buildings and equipment. The estate agent, Mr Preedy, ever-alert protector of Pym interests, wrote the usual letters of complaint. The request was made, for instance, that if the grounds were to be further used for reinforcement camps, then 'an alternative site be found for the Ablution Benches a little further away from the route which has to be taken by the female staff of the house'.

In early 1941, the Air Ministry finally took the action postponed in 1936, and began building an airfield on The Hazells' estate. They called it Tempsford Aerodrome and it was to play one of the most dramatic roles in the war. The new airfield was built about a mile and a half from the house, at the bottom of the hill. A row of magnificent elms was felled to create visibility for the runways, and temporary buildings were hastily put up to house the pilots, technicians and aircraft. Much of the village of Everton was occupied by WAAFs (the Women's Auxiliary Air Force), who made a very important contribution to the highly specialized and secret operations being conducted from the airfield. Barriers were put up around the aerodrome, and even the most naïve villager must have guessed that very high-level intelligence work was going on behind them.

The RAF now took over the Hall for use as the headquarters of two squadrons that had been assigned to work with the underground movement, or Maquis, flying by night from Tempsford into occupied France. Six Lysanders and two Hudsons shared these secret night-time 'special duties' from Tempsford. Pilots of one squadron dropped people and containers of ammunition, food and other equipment, not only over France but also later in the war over all of occupied Europe. The other squadron was also required to land its aircraft by night in some small secluded field, pick up one or more individuals or packages, and bring them back safely to England. At least 600 passengers were brought to England in this way – air force and military personnel, intelligence officers from S.O.E and M.I.9, and members of other underground organizations. Security was never breached, as far as anyone knows, although of course the Germans knew these activities were being carried on.

At first glance The Hazells might not have seemed the ideal spot for such a venture, since it is not close to the south coast. But for that very reason it was strategically desirable. It was far enough away not to be an obvious target, and yet not so far as to make flying distances any great challenge. Furthermore, the house itself was unusually problem-free. Fred Pym died in 1941. His heir, Leslie Pym, lived in Monmouthshire and spent most of his time in London as Member of Parliament, and Leslie Pym's son, Francis (now Lord Pym), was fighting in the Western desert, so there was no immediate family to move in. The RAF could have the run of the house, although they left a few rooms for the family to use.

In February 1943, Mr and Mrs Pym organized a major family event at The Hazells. They threw a twenty-first birthday party for their soldier son, inviting everyone from the village and the estate to tea to celebrate the occasion in his absence – a minor catering triumph in those days of rationing. A photograph was taken of this poignant event, showing the assembled company of well over a hundred people on the steps of the house.

One face in that astonishing crowd is that of Sir Robin Hooper, KCMG, DSO, DFC, whose wife's family were lifelong friends of the Pyms. Sir Robin was serving in the RAF and by coincidence had just been posted to The Hazells. 'My wife and parents-in-law came down for the party. We were looking round the house, and in the billiard room there was a long narrow table, on which parachutes were being folded and packed for the containers that were to be dropped into France. "What are those extraordinary things?" they asked me. Luckily I had only just arrived myself and could truthfully deny all knowledge!'

The house was used by senior officers and Squadron Leaders, which was apparently a mixed blessing. It was quite a long way from the airfield, so one either had to walk or hope to get a car, which was often not easy. Temporary buildings on the airfield, dispersed so as to diminish bombing effects, housed the canteen and planning stations. Gibraltar Farm, one of the estate farms, was where the 'Joes', or agents, were prepared for their daring night-journeys, dressed up as Frenchmen, strapped up in their parachute harnesses and checked to make sure no telltale piece of British identity or clothing (a crumpled bus ticket in a pocket, a cigarette stub) remained for the Gestapo to pounce on.

Sir Robin Hooper was one of the pilots (later a Squadron Leader), who started flying these missions in the winter of 1942. 'We were chosen because most of us spoke some French, but we were also supposed to have had some experience flying planes at night. You had to be capable of finding a field in the darkness about 300 miles into occupied France. Somebody just flashed a torch at you from the ground with a prearranged recognition letter, and you had to respond. The flare path was three pocket torches marking the little landing strip which was 150 metres with perhaps 400 in hand for emergencies.'

Tempsford was also used for radar jamming and secret transmissions into Europe, and later for regular bombing raids, but it was the feats of Sir Robin Hooper and his colleagues for which it will be remembered.

In 1945, after this particular war work was over at Tempsford, Leslie Pym suddenly died. When Francis Pym came back from the war, still in his early twenties, he faced a huge, empty house, traces of RAF occupation, and an uncertain future. There were double death duties, which was another burden on the young man. Although he was invited to buy back the Tempsford land by the Air Ministry, as requisitioned land was always offered back to the previous owners, thanks to the death duties he could not afford the price, and the land was purchased by his neighbour.

The RAF had left the house in reasonable condition, but Francis Pym knew he did not want to live at The Hazells, certainly not in the foreseeable future, and perhaps never. It had always seemed to him far too big for a family to live in. So the Pyms decided to let it for a period of years. Selling many of the interior furnishings, they put into storage in Bedford the most valuable furniture and paintings. About five years later the store went up in flames. 'That was really the *coup de grâce* for the house as far as the family was concerned.'

After being used as an annex to a mental hospital for twenty years, the condition of The Hazells deteriorated very seriously. Demolition was contemplated, but finally the house and its gardens were virtually given away to an architect for conversion into family residences. Now, happily, it has been restored and developed as separate houses and flats for twelve families, each with a private garden, and a share of the main gardens, which still largely resemble those Repton admired over a century earlier.

The war took few hostages from the landscape. There is a view from Everton where a hedge, low enough for the takeoff and landing of planes, runs along a ridge. Some locals remember the line of great elms that once rimmed that ridge. On the fields below the house, remnants of the main runway and a couple of hangars, now used as farm buildings, remain as modest monuments to a dramatic contribution to the country's history. Looking along the flat windswept fields, with The Hazells concealed over the brow of the hill, one can still imagine the sound of the Lysanders taking off by the light of the moon on their brave rescue missions to France nearly fifty years ago.

The Hospital,
The Air Force Billet
ASHTON WOLD

*'I don't think sufficient credit was given to the
American Air Force. They were magnificent.
We couldn't have won the war without them.'*

– The Hon. Miriam Rothschild Lane, 1987

Ashton Wold

ASHTON · NORTHAMPTONSHIRE

ASHTON WOLD IS a manor house situated at the end of a long, dark, muddy driveway, overgrown with shrubs and nettles, and lined with warnings such as 'Ramp', or 'Slow: Blind Dog', that never seem to materialize. Persist bravely up the shrouded, potholed drive and one comes to a circular front entrance that looks like something out of *Jane Eyre*, wild, unused, locked and bolted, unvisited. The stranger hastily retreats from this unwelcoming façade, and turns to the back, where cars, dogs and the paraphernalia of country life are gratefully in evidence.

This mysterious and romantic estate, built by Charles Rothschild at the beginning of this century, played an extraordinary dual role during World War Two. On the land was the Polebrooke airbase, where the Flying Fortresses made their dramatic and short-lived debut, and 6,000 Americans flew their dangerous missions over Europe. The house itself was a Red Cross Hospital. One small step from war to peace. 'I think that according to the Geneva Convention, this was illegal,' says Miriam Rothschild Lane, who grew up in Ashton Wold, by that time had inherited it, and single-handedly steered it through the war. 'Of course I had offered the house to the Red Cross long before there was any question of the airfield. But the war was a very funny thing. Nobody said anything. Here was a hospital right next door to an operational airfield. I don't suppose the Air Ministry ever knew.'

'What the Air Ministry Knew' might be the farcical title for much that went on in Ashton Wold in the early days of the war. 'Of course we were totally unprepared,' Mrs Lane remembers. 'When they came to lay down the airfield, they were working from old maps. Now it was my property and I wanted to help them. The first thing I saw was that the plan they made for laying their main cables ran straight through three rather large ponds. I asked them if there was any point in that. And they said, "No, we didn't know there were any ponds there." The ponds had been put in in 1900, so their maps must have been *very* old.'

Mrs Lane (or Miriam Rothschild as she then was) suggested better places for the cables, and that was how they were laid out. 'They wanted to build the women's quarters in a place which I told them was unsuitable because it was so wet. But they took no notice and when I went to see the WAAFs there were ducks swimming in their rooms.'

Because of the old maps, the Air Ministry people did not know there was a wood on the edge of the proposed airfield, so Mrs Lane had to give them permission to fell some of it, in order for aircraft to land more easily. 'I was my own agent at this time, so I was asked to put a value on the wood. I put a value on it of £2,000 which now of course seems absurdly low. I was supposed to receive this in compensation. Well, in the same post – I am not exaggerating – I received two letters. One was from a government department saying that it was noted that I'd valued the wood at £2,000, but that unfortunately this type of compensation could not be paid until after the war. The other envelope was from another government department, containing a £2,000 cheque for the wood!'

Finally the landing strips were done. At this time there was a serious scare of an invasion. 'I had qualified as a dairymaid,' recalls Mrs Lane, 'since there was nobody to milk the cows. I was also an air-raid warden. It so happened that the men of the Ordnance Corps were billeted in our stables, and the officers were in a house that normally belonged to one of the estate agents. I was in the habit of inviting these officers to lunch on Sunday.

'The day that Churchill went on the wireless warning us of the impending invasion, I thought: "I can't invite these officers to lunch, they'll be standing at the ready." So I went to find them to ask for their reactions, but they had all gone away for the weekend. But being rather officious, and a good air-raid warden, I thought: "I'd better go and see what has happened to the men, since we are expecting an invasion at any minute." So I drifted off with my gas mask into the stables and there was not a soul there. But all their rifles were on their beds. Well, in the Army you are not supposed to be separated from your rifle, particularly when you are expecting an invasion at any minute. So I collected all the rifles and took them into what was my gun room where we kept our sporting guns and carefully stacked them up and locked the door. Then I went home and had my lunch, expecting the invasion at any minute.

'There is a famous story about the telegram that went out at that time, saying, EXPECT THE INVASION FROM DUSK TO DAWN. Then a correction went out, FOR DUSK TO DAWN READ DAWN TO DUSK. So at Dawn the next day, the invasion hadn't come and the telephone rang. It was the Captain, who had returned and found his army without arms. He said, "Have you a-a-a . . ." He stammered on the phone, so I said, "You're looking for your rifles." And he said "Yes," so I unlocked their rifles and gave them back to him. I thought at the time, if we win the war it is an absolute miracle.'

Many extraordinary measures were taken during the period of expected invasion. Every village had to appoint a head man, who was given consignments of food to be stored, so that in case one was cut off and completely isolated, the head man could feed the village. Miriam Rothschild was of course appointed head man of Ashton, and when her food consignment came it was accompanied by an official letter which announced on the front, NOT TO BE OPENED UNTIL THE ENEMY IS WITHIN 10 MILES.

'So I thought, well, I'm not going to wait, I'll open it. So I opened the letter, and it said, "When the Germans are within ten miles, you are to round up the cattle and drive them into the church." I thought I would find out what the next village was going to do about this. The head man of the next village was also a woman, of course, so I went to see her, and asked, "I'm going to bury the food. Do you know how long tins last underground?" She had no idea, so then I said, "Did you get a letter too?" "Oh, yes," she said. So I said innocently, "What did it say?" And she said, "It said not to be opened until the Germans are within ten miles, and since I didn't want them to find it, I burned it." So I never found out whether she, also, had to round up the cattle!'

Nearly everyone in the country had to face the possibility of confrontation with the enemy. It was one of the more interesting private tests of conscience and political conviction. Miriam Rothschild was Jewish, and many of her family in Hungary had been sent to concentration camps. She had not a glimmer of a doubt. 'I decided that I would arm the village, because I had quite a lot of guns and rifles, and that I'd die with a rifle in my hand.' As for the food consignment, she and her secretary, the only person in her confidence, buried the tins in the wood and planted small trees on top, to explain the newly turned soil.

The tins have never been dug up. They must still be there.

One of the major contributions of Polebrooke airfield was that it was the first one to fly Flying Fortresses. 'These were the first planes we had seen in England which had vapour trails. This was very exciting to everybody.' The young Miriam Rothschild, as chatelaine of Ashton Wold, frequently invited the officers and pilots to dinner at her home, and got to know them well. 'There was no proper air conditioning in these planes, and the pilots had to go into decompression chambers built at the airfield to see if they could stand the altitude. The other great problem with the Flying Fortresses was that they were very big and heavy, and therefore difficult to land. They would discuss these problems with me, describing that to come down at the speed required to land on the runways was really very dicey. When these fellows came in the evening it was something they always talked about. We used to stay up talking and drinking till perhaps four in the morning.'

How the airmen must have enjoyed the civilized evenings with their lively and intelligent hostess. Many of them would then take off on a raid and never come back. 'I lost a lot of friends,' she says. 'It was an agonizing experience.'

When the Americans joined the British at the airbase in 1940, the 'marriage' seems to have been fairly harmonious, except for one thing. 'One of the grouses which reached me was that the American CO was sending the British off on all the really bloody missions. So the British were getting wiped out, not the Americans. I knew the CO very well by this time, and I told him what people were saying. "In a way it's true," he said. "My American boys are still green. They're not really broken into the war yet. For you British, it's a different thing. You're much tougher. Anyone who's been to Eton can stand anything."'

By the end of 1941, the British had left and 6,000 Americans were now in full charge of the airbase. 'The local people loved them. An added reason was that we were very short of luxury foods like sugar, and the Americans had an enormous amount of everything. If you asked them to dinner, they always came with a packet of sugar and a packet of this and that. They sometimes went too far, pulling handfuls of pound notes out of their pockets, inviting envy in the local villagers. But I feel they were never appreciated enough for their great sacrifices.'

The brave flyers were not the only ones to enjoy Miriam Rothschild's hospitality. Other, rather smaller members of society also found refuge at Ashton Wold.

'I've always been very interested in natural history, and particularly closely linked with the natural history side of the British Museum. So when the war broke out, and all the collections were split up to be sent away for safekeeping, I was assigned to house the Worm Collection at Ashton Wold. I organized its removal from London in a van, which had the misfortune to break down on the way and land up in a ditch, so the Worm Collection had a very bumpy ride. But it arrived safely and I arranged it in a room on the ground floor. I also acquired the curator of the worms, and then the curator's wife and the curator's daughter, so I had Worms Plus in one part of the house. It was one of the contributions of the war effort that we saved the Worm Collection from being bombed.'

The occupation of Ashton Wold by the worms was slightly less noticeable, of course, than the occupation by the Red Cross. 'Originally, they had wanted the hospital for officers, but I said no. My only stipulation was that it should be for private soldiers. One romantic result of this was that I met my husband.'

Miriam Rothschild had taken an intelligence post at Bletchley Park early in 1940, and had moved out of the house into the village. She spent the week at Bletchley, staying with her cousin, Lord Rosebery, at Mentmore Towers, returning to Northamptonshire at weekends.

'On a weekend leave I came to the house to see if it had burned down in my absence, and the commandant told me that there was a soldier at the hospital who claimed he had a letter from my mother. My poor mother died in May 1940, and this was considerably later, so I said, "It sounds very improbable. Who is he?"

'The commandant told me he was Hungarian, which made it less improbable, since my mother was Hungarian and always took a fantastic interest in anyone from that country. "He's going to lose an arm," the commandant told me. So I felt sorry, and went to see him. He was a very good-looking fellow, and he did produce a letter from my mother, which said "I was very interested in your article in the paper about refugees arriving at Harwich, and I'd very much like to meet you." He told me he'd forgotten all about the letter, because he'd volunteered and so on, and on the drive to the hospital with a wound in his arm he thought, "Ashton Wold, that rings a bell," and brought out the letter and there it was. And that's how we met. It was very romantic.'

At a time of intense emotional and physical stress, in a world almost unimaginable to those of us who regard it from this distance, such a meeting as that between Miriam Rothschild, a young woman working at the highest level of secret war operations, while her childhood home is alternately surrounded by aircraft and hospital personnel, and a handsome, courageous Hungarian refugee, thanks to a letter from the dead, seems the stuff of fiction.

'I married him in the middle of the war and we lived a very peculiar life. He joined the commandos, in a very special troop consisting only of Jewish refugees, and they had to be trained to be dropped behind enemy lines. We would be in bed at night and there'd be a knock on the door. "There's a raid on." And he would get up, dress, and we never knew if we would see each other again. It was hectic, and very traumatic. I don't know how I survived it.'

One of the distractions at Ashton during the American occupation was the visit of famous Americans, a propaganda effort to show how everyone was partaking in the war effort. Film stars such as Clark Gable, James Stewart and Margaret Whiting all turned up at Ashton, to boost the troops' morale. Needless to say, Miriam Lane was in the thick of the fray.

'The first evening Clark Gable arrived, the CO rang up and asked if he could bring him to dinner, and I said, "Of course." Then I thought, he must be so bored always being asked for his autograph, I must think up something else. So I gave him a photograph of myself, aged four, signed, milking a cow. He wasn't a bit amused. Not a bit. During dinner I asked him, "Who are the rising stars of the cinema?" "There are no stars except me." He said that quite seriously.'

If Gable lacked a sense of humour, he was a marvellous shot. Miriam and he used to go out together in the evening with a .22 rifle to shoot rooks. Two excellent shots, the famous American film idol and the young woman scientist, prowling through the woods after rooks in the English twilight – an irresistible vignette of wartime.

Gable also contributed to one of the more entertaining moments on the base. 'They used to give dances and parties at the airfield, with a few carefully selected local girls. Clark Gable invited me up to one of these parties, and he asked if I'd like to dance. Now in the tent there was a buffet set up, and every so often there was a bowl of castor sugar which you were supposed to use for your coffee. I have a very sweet tooth, and I said, "No, frankly, what I'd like to do is sit down there and eat a bowl of sugar."

'So I sat down and started eating the sugar. Suddenly I felt there was tension in the air. I looked round and saw Clark Gable poised on the edge of his chair just about to dive into the back of the tent, and around him was a circle of nurses who had come from the hospital ready to debag him. The one idea was to get a piece of his underwear as a souvenir. He had to run for his life – leaving me there eating the sugar.'

Although Ashton, in the centre of England, was on the path of many German raids, particularly on Coventry, not a single bomb fell on the airfield. The only bombs to fall were practice bombs, dropped by American trainee pilots. 'Almost 350 bombs fell off target,' Miriam Lane recalls ruefully, 'including through the roof of my garage. There were two or three occasions when I had to lie in a ditch for hours not to be killed by our own side! One day when they started high-level bombing practice, I crawled out of my ditch and got to the phone and rang up the CO and said, "You must stop the bastards bombing me out of house and home." And he said, "Mrs Lane, we've tried to get hold of them to stop them but we can't!" That was how chaotic everything was.'

This erratic, unnatural, nerve-tingling existence at Ashton Wold came to an end in 1945. The Red Cross moved out, the Americans went home, the airfield ceased to be operational. Various efforts were made to restore it to some kind of function on the estate, but the battle-scarred soil resisted, and now the obsolete landing strips are overgrown with wildflowers, in happy recognition of one of Miriam Lane's post-war passions.

Few other traces of the war remain. There is a piece of land on the airfield, donated by the Lanes, on which the US Air Force erected a memorial to their dead, preserving a piece of the original runway as an addition to the monument. The top floor of the house, where all the hospital beds were installed, was removed by Mrs Lane's son, to whom she had made over the property. The worms and their curator went back to London. The Hungarian pilot came home safely after being a prisoner of war, and took up residence as husband and father at Ashton Wold.

Wandering through the calm, fairy-tale village and down the winding driveway to the remote manor house, one can hardly believe what went on during those six wild, hilarious, tragic years. Nothing now disturbs the rural silence. No bombers, no soldiers, no nurses, no sirens, no blackout. Only the irresistible feeling of time having drawn a veil over those tumultuous days, of a healed landscape begging to be left in peace.

The Hospital
HEATH HOUSE

*'Wherever they went, when they
returned to the Front, they always
knew they could come back to us.'*
– Margaret, Countess of Lichfield, 1987

Heath House

TEAN · STAFFORDSHIRE

 MOST OF THE STORIES of these country houses can be told only in human terms, and nowhere is it more true than in the case of Heath House, where the tale is not only of individual dedication, but also of faith and miracles.

Born in 1899, Violet Margaret Fawson Greene was brought up in Whittington Hall, North Lancashire, in a standard of feudal luxury (Romneys on the wall, footmen, private trains) that is now chronicled by students of sociology with a kind of breathless awe. This idyll was shattered by a series of rapid-fire consecutive tragedies endemic to the age – her father's premature death in 1912 aged forty-nine from an unsuccessful operation, the loss of her twenty-year-old brother, the heir, in the First World War, and the death of her elder sister from complications following the birth of her first child.

Defeated by the accumulation of triple death duties, Violet Margaret was forced to sell the much-loved family home. After marriage to Humphrey Philips she moved to his house, Oak Hill, near Tean, Staffordshire, where she bore him two sons. When the Second World War broke out the RAF requisitioned Oak Hill and she moved into her father-in-law's house nearby in Heybridge. In 1941 she found herself Commandant of a hospital based in the home of her cousin-by-marriage, Anthony Philips. Heath House, Tean, near Stoke-on-Trent, was her home and centre of her life's work for the next four years.

Heath House was built by John Burton Philips, scion of a Staffordshire family dating back to the mid-sixteenth century. Begun in 1836 on the site of an earlier house, its architecture is typical of the mid-Victorian grand Tudor/Gothic style, rather daunting in demeanour, but a family house none-theless, having remained in Philips hands for over three hundred years. 'Lady Dorothy Meynell [head of the Staffordshire Red Cross] requisitioned the house,' recently recalled the Commandant, Margaret, Countess of Lichfield just before her death in 1988. 'She knew all the houses in the county extremely well. She was a first cousin of my husband's. She just told me I was going to be the Commandant, and that was that!'

Lady Lichfield had lived through the First World War, her own home being requisitioned for an officer's hospital. 'I was mostly in the basement doing the washing up,' she says. 'But having been in the First World War, when the second one came, it was like getting back into old shoes. I had been working with the Red Cross for years. You ran your hospital your own way.'

The newly appointed Commandant indeed ran it her own way. Keeping her own quarters at Heybridge, with a modest staff, she travelled every morning the three miles to Heath House, her first task being to get it in shape for patients. 'There was a terrible frost that first winter of the war. Finally a lorry arrived with fifty-five iron hospital beds which were dumped in the stables. Fifty-five mattresses went into the garages. Then the lorry left, without telling anyone. I found everything quite by chance. Well, I had no help then. And it was very slippery. But I carried the beds into the house by myself – all fifty-five of them, on my head.'

She advertised in *The Times* for Red Cross people to help in the hospital. The response was gratifying. 'All my staff were very good. Only one had to be fired for kissing patients in the bushes.' One of the respondents was Peggy Whittall, whose family was in Turkey and whose fiancé had been taken prisoner. She became assistant and personal secretary to the 'Com', the name everyone called Mrs Philips. Many years later she described the routine for 'the Com's army' at Heath House: 'We were up at seven, and before breakfast I had to clean out half a dozen grates and re-lay and light the fires. Then came breakfast and the endless performance of washing up, rinsing up and drying up. The Com was a perfectionist. The glasses had to shine, the cutlery and plates were inspected and often rejected by her. The tea towels were washed after every meal. It is remarkable, looking back now, that a woman who had never had to do anything before, should know exactly what had to be done and how to do it.'

The Com's patients were enlisted men only, and came from all over England. Some of them were very badly hurt. One had a tin stomach. Others had shell-shock. 'With one pair, I would make them take it in turns reading to each other to help them come back to life. Their eyes were dead.' The invalids would stay at Heath House for two or three weeks and then return to their units and to the war.

While Heath House itself was no more nor less sympathetic a place than many other country houses converted into hospitals, and the nursing standards perhaps no higher than at these other places, something very special was offered to the men at Heath House. For the Com was no ordinary Commandant. Not only did she have a terrific sense of humour (laughter was one of the most vivid memories for those who stayed there), but she cared as much, if not more, for those men who passed through her hands as for her own two sons, both fighting in the war.

'No Englishman of that class, I don't think, would ever own to fear. But they used to come and talk to me about the war, and about their experiences. Every morning when I arrived, there would be a handful of the men waiting in the dark passage to see me, and we would go into my office and talk a little and I would try to cheer them up. Then they would leave. They had to go back to the war, we all knew that. Those awful goodbyes . . .

'They were often very frightened, of course. The Colonel posted to us from Trentham was a Scotsman, and we both felt we had a kind of second sight. When our patients left us, we could always tell when they were in trouble. You can get in contact with people spiritually, when they depend on you. The Colonel, being in the Army, would check and find one of them was missing. Then we would both go out into the garden and pray.

'One of our men had suffered a blow which had cracked his skull. He had the most appalling agony in his head, because his skull was pressing on his brain. But to get that right with an operation could have done more harm than good. Now I'm a complete amateur at healing but I used to go on walks in the garden with the patients on their own, so they could talk and get things off their chests. We had these gorgeous woods at Heath House, with rhododendrons and azaleas, and wonderful rides. At the end of one of the rides was a temple, with pillars, steps and a dome. The view from this temple was out of this world, across the whole of England.

'So one afternoon I took the man with the fractured skull out with me and said to him, "Look at this, really take it in. Drink it in with body and soul because this is really heaven on earth. This would make a wonderful place to make an act of faith. To God. It's very simple. Just say "Please." He was rather touching. He took off his hat and went down on one knee and made an act of faith. Then he got up and we walked back through the rhododendrons, and I sent him off to tea and went to sign some letters. And then I went home.

'The next morning there were lots of men outside my door waiting to see me, and as the passage was so dark I could never see who it was standing there, so I would say good morning to them all. And I had about three men in my room when suddenly the door burst open and a man I was sure I had never seen before said, "Look, look! It's me! I woke up in the night and a great pair of hands came and picked up my head and took away the pain! I haven't got any more pain!"'

This story is typical of the spirit of Heath House, a spirit that informs the memories of those who worked there, and leaps off the pages of the Visitors Books, letters and postcards from gunners, bombardiers, privates and corporals, kept and treasured by Lady Lichfield all these years. 'The spirit of service' was one of her favourite expressions, but it was surely more than that. In the Visitors Books she kept notes of all the arrivals. 'Came from Orkneys suffering from rheumatism and fearful cough (anti-aircraft)'; or 'Crashed in plane.' The patients then wrote their comments: 'Another home to go to!' 'I envy those that follow.' 'Lovely place and lovely crowd, I'll have to try and go bad again . . .'

Countless letters came to her from former patients returned to the Front in Europe, Egypt, the Far East, clumsily-written notes filled with gratitude and nostalgia for a moment's peace and happiness in the midst of the horrors of death. 'Wars are not nice, Commandant, but I will always be grateful to this war, for giving me the opportunity of spending a little time with some of the finest people in the world.' The contrast between the two worlds made one corporal write: 'When I think of the delightful days I spent at Heath House, sitting in the sun, or playing tennis, it rather tends to make one bitter. Because all the time I was convalescing at Heath House, people were being hunted and tortured by the Gestapo.'

They also wrote poems. It is difficult to imagine anything at that time (or indeed any time) inspiring young, poorly-educated working-class soldiers to the composition of poetry, but here is a small portion of a fourteen-verse epic called 'Christmas Day at Heath House, 1944':

'The Commandant's Speech, by no means a bore,
Included Red Cross, some Religion and more.
Throats were kept moistened with lashings of beer,
And many a toast was drunk with good cheer.'

Another poet wrote a long tribute to Heath House, which included the lines:

'What sort of place is this, thought I,
Another place to come and die.
But from the moment I entered the house,
I had no need to grumble and grouse.
I met the Commandant who wore a smile and a grin,
And for me a new life was to begin . . .
Who knows how the Commandant and her staff worked it,
For they certainly made a man of Bombardier Birkett.'

It certainly wasn't the interior of Heath House that provoked such feeling. Much of it was boarded up and furniture removed to storage. 'The paintings and furniture remaining in the house bored them stiff. It wasn't their cup of tea at all. Since country houses have been opened to the public, there has been a tremendous education about art and furniture. In those days they were completely ignorant. But they were marvellous. No damage whatsoever was done. Many of the wallpapers are still there now.

'They were good about the blackout, and used to go outside to see if any light was showing. We had no air raid shelters to bother about. We were in the middle of nowhere in rural Staffordshire, and it would have been bad luck if a bomb had fallen, that's all. Most Englishmen are gardeners, and they loved the gardens. But they never knew the names of plants and after a while they asked if they might be labelled. And in the end they did it themselves!'

The spirit of Heath House, like the Com, had a religious foundation, and there was always a service on Sunday in the library. 'They had communion whether they had been confirmed or not because our chaplain thought it a good thing. And they had never seen anything like it. "Wafer? Wot do you do with this? Put it in yer pocket?" But I think it helped them. It was something new.' Peggy Whittall describes those Sundays with Padre Best:

'His sermons were invariably unprepared and came straight from the heart. The services took place in the Library and he would gaze at the glorious view through the French windows and tell us remarkable stories of valour at Gallipoli. He would get so carried away with his thoughts of the distant past that quite unobtrusively he would slide his bottom onto the altar, make himself comfortable and reach for his pipe, then pat his pockets to find his matches.

'The Com would start to fidget in the front row while I subsided in a fit of giggles. In a flash matches were striking up in the back rows and the patients by now were all smoking. The Com would repeat sternly, with an ever-increasing crescendo, "Padre. PADRE" – until at last he returned to us from Gallipoli and hastily put away his pipe.'

The Com was spiritual adviser, confidante and social worker to her patients. She willingly took on their personal and family problems, and helped these poor inexperienced young men sort out their lives as best she could, knowing that when they returned to the Front they might never come back. One gunner's wife ran off with a married man with eight children. The gunner had invested his savings in his wife's name. She left without an address. The Com arranged for her patient to apply for free legal advice. She wrote on this occasion: 'He is a very honest, nice man and I do hope that the Legal Advice Bureau will be able to help him . . . It is very bad for him to have this worry on his mind while he is hanging about in Hospital . . .'

Another gunner got a young woman pregnant while on leave in London. Unfortunately he also had a wife and four children in Cheshire. The pregnant girl came to Heath House to see him, demanding that he take proper responsibility for her and the child and leave his wife. The Com told him he must confess all to his wife, which he did. The Com continued to help by corresponding with the wife in Cheshire, persuading her to forgive her husband. 'Your husband has talked to me a good deal about the future,' she wrote. 'I agree with you that your husband is very easily led, which is his great weakness . . . He has had a pretty good eye-opener to the appalling mistake that he had made, and I think he has learned his lesson.' She also counselled the pregnant girl, urging her to accept that a marital reconciliation was much the best resolution to the problem.

Heath House Auxiliary Hospital opened in April 1941 and closed in December 1945. During that time, 1,412 service patients passed through the hospital. Their letters and poems are testimony to the extraordinary sense of well-being they experienced while convalescing there. Whereas for many wartime Commandants (mostly county ladies), their patients were faceless numbers in hospital beds, installed for a few weeks and then gone for ever, for Margaret Philips they were living, suffering human beings, and she attended to all of them.

'Those days should not be lost to history,' she said. 'For goodness and kindness shine out from them like a Lighthouse in the storm of destruction.

The Red Cross and St John's Ambulance were saviours in times of suffering. Our lovely historical houses and their gardens added to their history in the healing of men in mind, body and soul, when for a while they came out of hell and found themselves in heaven.'

The Hospital
RAGLEY HALL

*'We didn't have any regular lookouts for
bombs. I think my mother and my nanny
went up on the roof sometimes to see if
they could see anything.'*

– The Marquess of Hertford, 1987

Ragley Hall

ALCESTER · WARWICKSHIRE

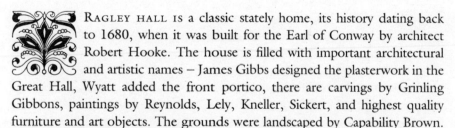 RAGLEY HALL IS a classic stately home, its history dating back to 1680, when it was built for the Earl of Conway by architect Robert Hooke. The house is filled with important architectural and artistic names – James Gibbs designed the plasterwork in the Great Hall, Wyatt added the front portico, there are carvings by Grinling Gibbons, paintings by Reynolds, Lely, Kneller, Sickert, and highest quality furniture and art objects. The grounds were landscaped by Capability Brown.

Yet this treasury of decorative arts was offered without hesitation, as were so many others, to the war effort. Ragley was a hospital in both world wars; in the second, the present Marquess of Hertford's mother was Commandant (and also president of the local Red Cross). Her son was nine years old at the time and brings a unique perspective to those war years at Ragley.

'My mother had recently been widowed and had the task, with the help of the estate staff, of packing everything up and putting it all away. The Study and the Library were used by Mother and by my sister and myself when we were at home, so they remained untouched. The Great Hall had fifty beds put into it. The Louis XVI furniture in the Red Drawing Room stayed put as it was used as the nurses' sitting room. The Green Drawing Room and the Prince Regent's Bedroom were cluttered up with furniture and pictures and shut up completely. The Red Drawing Room and the Anteroom were filled up with beds. The Dining Room was the recreation room. All the silver was taken away to two separate bank vaults in remote country villages to be safe from bombing. It didn't return until my wife and I moved into the house after we married in 1956.

'The hospital wasn't very glamorous. It was specifically for people with skin diseases, mainly caused by wearing khaki. Quite a lot of people apparently were allergic to the dye used in army clothing and they came here to get over it. Then I suppose they had to be shifted into some occupation that doesn't require the wearing of khaki, like the RAF, perhaps! Including patients and staff and our family, there were about 100 people in the house altogether. My nanny's sister, who had been my grandmother's parlourmaid, came here at the start of the war and found herself cooking for all 100 people. She was marvellous.

'I only went into the side of the house that was used as a hospital when there was a party in the recreation room, like an ENSA concert. Sometimes I remember there were dances. I was taught to dance by the matron of the hospital. She was a tiny little woman and made me waltz with very short steps, which was rather good for me, actually. Waltzing remains my only contribution to the dancefloor. Unfortunately it is not a very popular one, as nobody seems to waltz these days.

'As a child, I rather enjoyed the war. A lot of my cousins were also staying here, relations who had been evacuated from the coast, and when the air raid sirens went we were all taken downstairs into the basement where big sofas had been installed, including one that's in the library now. We used to sleep there, which of course was much more exciting than sleeping in your own bed. We spent quite a lot of time looking for German spies in the grounds. And I used to play tennis with the patients when they were getting better. The patients had the run of the gardens, which were kept up. I think we always had at least two gardeners, which was fortunate.'

At the end of the war, the future of Ragley Hall was seriously threatened by a series of inheritance crises. Lord Hertford's grandfather had disinherited his eldest son, leaving the Ragley Estate, reduced by death duties to 12,000 acres, in trust to his second son, Lord Hertford's father, Lord Henry Seymour. Unfortunately, Lord Henry died in 1939, and his elder brother in 1940, leaving triple death duties to be borne by the nine-year-old heir. The estate was reduced to 6,000 acres and was all let to tenant farmers except for 1,000 acres of woodland.

Lord Hertford and his mother moved into a farmhouse, and the Trustees embarked on plans to sell Ragley to a firm of demolition contractors. But the young Marquess fought to save the house, and after his marriage moved back in with his wife, and began the arduous process of restoration. 'My mother never had much sense of the value of things. The Crown Derby bowls tended to get used for the dogs, a rare Meissen dish for fruit salad, and so on. But all the best china had been put in crates and stored in the basement, along with many of the paintings. Ironically, they were the only ones that got damaged – because of the damp. Bits of gold leaf kept flaking off the frames. We spent a very long time unpacking those crates. Afterwards, my mother-in-law gave us a book on early china in which she had inscribed, "In memory of seventeen crates." '

Ragley Hall is now in fine shape, lived in by the Hertford family, and open to the public. The only aftermath of its wartime role is that even now treasures still get discovered. 'My mother had packed up everything pretty well except that there were three beautiful golden snuff boxes that she stored in a safe place and after the war she couldn't remember where she'd put them. We didn't find them for twenty-one years!'

Treasure Repository
BOUGHTON HOUSE

*'Our people are fortunate in many ways in
being billeted on a Duke.'*

– Sir John Forsdyke, Director of
the British Museum, June 1941

Boughton House

NR KETTERING · NORTHAMPTONSHIRE

On 22 July 1933, the Trustees of the British Museum met to discuss the safe custody of British national art treasures in time of war. At that time Hampton Court was one of the Museum's favourite candidates to serve as a repository. Although it was not far from London, it would serve as a convenient temporary storehouse awaiting the gradual removal to country houses further from the city. Moving roomfuls of mummies was evidently not something the Trustees felt could be tackled overnight. 'It was certain that any future war would open with massed air attacks, and that there would not again be the time for preparation of sandbags, etc., that there was in 1914–1918.'

The question was raised whether it was wise to concentrate all material in one spot. The alternative most favourably considered was that each museum or department should remove its material to previously selected houses or institutions. The Trustees directed that the Office of Works be furnished with a schedule of packing cases required. In December of that year the Museum agreed to prepare schedules of the most precious objects, with a view to rapid removal in case of a threat to war, and a list of recommended houses was to be drawn up by the Ministry of Works.

In the years before 1939, most institutions, art galleries and museums met

145

to discuss these same matters that concerned the Trustees of the British Museum, and began making preparations to store their treasures in places outside the probable war zone. By the outbreak of war, the National Gallery had already dispersed 2,000 pictures to houses such as Avening, in Gloucestershire, Penrhyn Castle, and Crosswood near Aberystwyth, and to the National Library of Wales and the University of Wales. The Tate Gallery collection was sent to Muncaster Castle, Ravenglass, Cumberland, Hellens, Much Marcle, Hereford-shire, and Eastington Hall, Worcestershire. As bombing raids spread, the works of art from Much Marcle and Eastington were sent to what was regarded as a safer sanctuary at Sudeley Castle. The owners of these houses remained in residence, with guards day and night for their unusual visitors.

Montacute House was the repository for many of the Victoria and Albert Museum collections, but probably it was Mentmore, home of Lord Rosebery, that had the most varied treasures consigned to its capacious rooms. The Marchioness of Crewe, Lord Rosebery's sister, who stayed at Mentmore during the war, remembers wandering through the house and finding the central hall 'filled with historic ceilings from Greenwich and Marlborough House and the floor of the Billiards Room covered with the recumbent figures of kings and queens from Westminster Abbey ... I used to walk outdoors past the Maze, flanked by huge bushes of sweet-smelling syringa, till I came to the summit of a slope and there, gazing over the view of the orchards that lay below, was the romantic equestrian figure of Charles I by Le Sueur, removed from London for safety.'

By the middle of 1938, Boughton House, Drayton House and Deene Park, all in what was regarded as the relatively safe county of Northamptonshire, had been settled on as suitable places to store material from the British Museum. In the end, Deene was requisitioned by the military, absorbing six different units between 1940 and 1944, including Greeks, Poles and Indians, but for the other two houses, their role as treasure repository was assured. The owners were certainly not going to object. Once these houses were earmarked on the Central Register, they were ineligible for requisitioning by the War Department. The Buccleuch art collections were thus saved from the military. (Other Buccleuch houses were less fortunate. Drumlanrig got off lightly as quarters for St Denis's, a leading girls' school from Edinburgh, and Dalkeith House, just outside Edinburgh, turned into a barracks for the military, including sections of the Polish Army, suffered only superficial damage, but Bowhill, in Selkirkshire, was badly damaged and most of Langholm Lodge in Dumfriesshire had to be destroyed.)

The present Duke of Buccleuch has his own theory as to why Boughton was on the British Museum list. 'My grandfather died in 1936 and, in their efforts to grab everything they could, the Inland Revenue employed museum officials to scour every inch of our houses with a view to extracting the maximum amount of death duties that they could. This may have resulted in a lot of people who took decisions about evacuation knowing about Boughton House at first hand.' The Duke also mentions with a certain wry pleasure, 'There were two officials who would, I believe, have given it a clear berth if they could. These two had been charged with the task of valuing a large number of items which were being stored in the Library in 1937–38 and they were so affected by powerful feelings of somebody glaring at them over their shoulders that they fled the house, abandoning much of their task.'

A special Standing Commission of the British Museum Subcommittee on Air Raid Precautions, at the National Museums and Galleries, under the central authority of the Office of Works, met in February 1939, to deal with emergency accommodations and to evaluate the suitability of the country houses recommended for evacuation. Each institution was to decide when evacuation should begin.

Some museums seem to have found it more difficult than others to face up to the realities this entailed, as Miriam Rothschild relates.

'During the summer of 1938 I sought an interview with the late Dr Foster Cooper who was then director of the Natural History Museum, and I discussed my deep apprehension. Would it not be a good idea to have a plan of action ready for dispersing the collections about the country, I asked. I elaborated this plan: The owners of large country houses would welcome such a proposal because little if any damage would result from storage of collections compared to that inflicted, for instance, by military occupation. Furthermore large estates were usually equipped with well-sprung shooting brakes, which could help with transport. Dr Foster Cooper thanked me for calling on him and then smiled kindly: "But dear lady," he said, "since there will be no war – let us talk of something more interesting."

'I decided after that, notwithstanding the snub, to elaborate the plan, and I contacted the owners of several large stately homes and found them enthusiastic and most cooperative. I therefore wrote a report to the Chairman of the Trustees, with concrete suggestions for a scheme for evacuation of the collections if war was declared. The Chairman replied in his own handwriting, thanking me for my suggestions, but voicing the opinion that no plan was necessary at the present time.

'When a year later war was declared, absolutely nothing had been done about the evacuation of these priceless collections, nor was any action taken during the so-called "phoney war", when no air raids occurred. Apparently this lull-before-the-storm reassured the museum staff, who were now convinced that London would never be raided from the air.

'Then suddenly air raids began and a bomb or two fell near the museum destroying part of the building and with it some valuable collections. Considerable damage was done as usual by water from the fire hoses. Among the specimens lost was my father's collection of the genus iris. (Fortunately a duplicate collection was housed at Ashton and is now safely in the Herbarium at the Royal Botanic Gardens at Kew.) I returned to the museum next morning and sought out Dr Foster Cooper. I assured him that the plan to evacuate the collections was still viable and by the Grace of God there was perhaps still time. But the director was obviously in a state of deep shock and he could not or would not reply.

'There was a brilliant member of the staff, Dr Theresa Clay (who specialized in the study of bird lice), who was as worried as I was about the danger to the collections. We discussed the situation and she suggested we should both travel down to Aylesbury and put the matter before James de Rothschild, a cousin of mine who at that time was a junior minister. I immediately agreed and we found James extremely sympathetic. After considering the various points we put to him, he decided we must seek an audience with the Archbishop of Canterbury who was a Trustee of the British Museum. He arranged an interview for us – via the good offices of Secretary White-Thompson – the following day.

'Theresa and I were ushered into a panelled room in Lambeth Palace. The Archbishop was standing in the window and turned round slowly and looked at us coldly. He asked us what right we thought we had to interfere with museum affairs . . . he was a formidable man with a marvellous flow of smooth, biting censure. He was clearly outraged. I tried to explain, but I fumbled and hesitated – had it not been for the silent Theresa's grimly determined expression I think I would have bolted from the room.

'Finally, the Archbishop said acidly, "We have perfect confidence in the Director of our choice." I felt desperate. "The Director," I said, "is suffering from shell shock and it is a symptomatic but depressing fact that he is making a collection of 'bomb splinters' instead of evacuating the collections. He actually showed them to me with considerable pride . . ."

I saw the Archbishop start, but he coldly waved us out of the door.

' "Well," said Theresa sadly, "I admire you for struggling on."

' "Crushed," I said. "Flattened. Pulped . . ."

'At 9.00 am next day the Archbishop swept into the Natural History

Museum. I would have given a very great deal to be a mouse in the wainscott
... That afternoon the evacuation of the collections began. The cabinets
containing the preserved Helmmiths (parasitic worms) were taken by van to
Ashton, where they spent an uneventful war in a dry cellar.'

The British Museum finally plumped for 24 August 1939, to evacuate the
major contents of the Museum and Library to the assigned repositories –
Boughton, Drayton, and the National Library of Wales at Aberystwyth.
The Director of the Museum, Sir John Forsdyke, informed the Standing
Commission on 14 October 1939 that some 3,300 packing cases and materials
had been held in readiness for nearly a year for the evacuation. Furthermore,
Sir John was able to report that 'by the end of the first day ten tons of books,
manuscripts, prints and drawings had been despatched to the National Library
of Wales at Aberystwyth, twelve tons of perishable antiquities to Boughton
House and Drayton House, and a quantity of imperishable antiquities (not
affected by damp) to the Tube Railway Tunnel at Aldwych Station. Reception
parties in charge of Deputy Keepers were also sent to the various repositories.

'On the second day, twelve and a half tons of coins, twelve tons of perishable
antiquities and fifteen tons of Library material were despatched by rail. By
noon on the third day the whole collection of coins and medals had been
removed and the most valuable material of every Department was in safety.'

This smooth description hardly did justice to the astonishingly complicated
procedures that the Keepers and their staffs actually had to follow. Charts
showing the whereabouts of individual boxes had to be drawn up, priority lists
for salvage purposes completed, packing meticulously monitored, temperatures
carefully watched. Lorries and trains were both used for transportation, causing
their own problems. For deliveries to Drayton, for instance, special low-
wheeled lorries were required in order to clear the low outer gateway of the
house. One such lorry duly arrived, but when the container was unloaded the
springs of the lorry rose and they could not get the lorry back through the
gate again.

A consignment from Westminster Abbey was also added to the Museum's
deliveries to Boughton, including eight royal sepulchral figures in bronze
and wood, fifteen pictures and a retable. (The Westminster effigies went to
Mentmore.) The Museum staff stationed at Boughton, in their report back to
head office, pointed out that, 'it is a very large house, but unlived-in, in
parts highly inflammable, with two not very adequate external hydrants, and
containing only a skeleton staff of four domestics'. (For this reason Drayton
was easier, in that it was lived in with a full indoor staff.) The report also
mentions the difficulties of the removal at the London end. 'Since at no time

was there certainty of more than a few hours, freedom from air attack, it was necessary to plan the packing like a retreat, withdrawing the collections now from one gallery, now from another, as each became the most important part of the collection remaining.'

A year later the Museum staff at Boughton braced for another ordeal. Having finally settled in, in late 1940, they learned that an aerodrome was going to be constructed one mile away from Boughton, and that the collections would therefore have to be moved to a safer location. (The aerodrome was for the 8th US Army Air Force 384th Bombardment Group.) Meanwhile, the Air Ministry was vigorously advocating the dispersal of the material stored in the National Library of Wales, owing to the dangers of enemy aircraft. The Marquess of Northampton offered them Compton Wynyates in Warwickshire as an alternative, but the Air Ministry expressed doubts as to this house's eligibility, since it was in a 'crowded area' in respect of wireless navigational beams. The Government had also promised the Trustees, at their increasingly anxious urging, an air-conditioned underground accommodation at a stone quarry in Westwood, near Corsham, Wiltshire, that they were to share with the Victoria and Albert Museum, but it was not yet ready. (Most of the National Gallery art had already been removed to the Manod Slate Quarry in North Wales, where the Ministry of Works had constructed air-conditioned chambers 300 feet deep into the mountainside to store the works of Titian, Rubens, Michelangelo and other priceless masterpieces.)

At a meeting in the spring of 1941, owing to the doubts raised about Compton Wynyates, the Director finally decided not to vacate Boughton entirely, but to move two-thirds of the Boughton material to Compton Wynyates, and leave the rest where it was. Thus the collection of coins and medals, for instance, which had all been stored at Boughton, was now divided between Boughton, Compton Wynyates, and Drayton.

To move the treasures yet again was pretty well the last straw for the frailer members of the Museum staff, in particular Sidney Smith, Keeper of the department of Egyptian and Assyrian Antiquities, whose distress was made very clear to the Trustees. Of 748 boxes or packages at Boughton, he reported, 85 were fit for transport to Compton Wynyates with minor risk; 614 containing Cuneiform tablets and papyri he was not sure about. Of the remaining 49 he considered the contents so fragile that movement must be avoided at all costs. He was worried, not only about the responsibility of moving these priceless objects, but also about his own personal blame should any damage take place. Writing to a colleague he declared despairingly, 'From our point of view the best thing that can happen now is for the Hun to immobilize everything;

which is, I fear, precisely what will *not* happen.'

The Trustees might well have also preferred this solution at this point in the war. They were moving material from Boughton to Compton Wynyates, and from the National Library in Wales to Skipton Castle in Yorkshire. They were embarking on building a tunnel under the National Library in Aberystwyth in response to the Air Ministry's warnings, but the work was frustratingly slow. As well as these headaches, they had to contemplate the fact that the Medal Room in London had been completely destroyed by fire during an air raid in May 1941, and that further damage was to be expected.

In the end they decided to move half Mr Smith's department to Compton Wynyates and to Drayton, leaving the tomb-paintings, soft stone sculpture, and boxes containing the heaviest objects at Boughton. (Perhaps kindly, they also relieved the Keeper of his responsibilities in connection with the removal of his departmental material.) The Duke of Buccleuch was not sorry to see so much of the Museum's holdings go. 'In the blackout one stumbled over mummies of incredible rarity.'

But Boughton remained a major player in the Museum's game of musical antiquities. The destruction of the Medal Room, and shortly afterwards much of the South-West Quadrant of the Museum, confirmed the view that everything possible should be taken out of London. So while many treasures were leaving, others were arriving. A 3-ton Pickford's van, for instance, loaded with Far Eastern Printed Books, left London for Boughton in the summer of 1941. Furthermore, the Ministry of Works requested the Director of the Museum whether they would take at Boughton the painted panels from the House of Commons. 'They are in large frames about fifteen by ten feet, but I do not suppose that they will take much floor space,' Sir John wrote to his man at Boughton. 'If we are going to share the remaining accommodation with anybody, the Ministry of Works comes first. They have always done us very well.' Boughton was also borrowed by the Science Museum, who, as the Duke of Buccleuch recalls, 'decided anything was better than staying in London and brought large quantities of glass cases containing models of ships which were more agreeable companions than mummies'.

Other houses also continued to play their part in the British Museum's continued evacuations. Nearly 500 boxes of prints, drawings and manuscripts were removed to the care of the Earl of Crawford at Haigh Hall near Wigan, and of Captain E. G. Spencer Churchill at Northwick Park, near Bristol. Materials that could not go into the new tunnel under the National Library in Wales went to Skipton Castle.

By the spring of 1942, the Westwood Quarry was finished, and the rest of the antiquities at Boughton, Drayton and Compton Wynyates were removed there, where they remained until the end of the war. Only one slight accident occurred in the move from Boughton to Westwood. Two of the Egyptian tomb paintings were damaged, owing to the breaking of a rope which bound them to the side of the railway van. The reaction of Keeper Sidney Smith to this news is not recorded.

Secret Operations
CLAREMONT HOUSE

'It is not surprising that all the poets, and many others, who have had the privilege of visiting Claremont in the past, expressed their appreciation of its beauties in verse. Who will write its dirge?'

– Benton Fletcher, *Royal Homes Near London*, 1930

Claremont House

ESHER · SURREY

CLAREMONT AND ITS grounds have a complex architectural and social history. The story is worth relating in some detail since what happened here over the years has an ironic bearing on the house's role in World War Two. Originally built by Vanbrugh for his own use, Claremont was sold to the Duke of Newcastle in 1714, who enjoyed it until his death in 1768. The Duke took a great interest in the gardens, with various famous designers taking a hand in shaping the 300-plus acres. Charles Bridgeman made the original pond. William Kent enlarged it into a lake and added a grotto, as well as planting trees and creating vistas in the newly-fashionable landscape style.

On the Duke of Newcastle's death the estate was bought by Clive of India, who promptly demolished the house and invited Capability Brown to build a new one on a better, higher site. This was a great assignment for Brown, for whom (as for most landscape architects) designing a house and landscape together was the ideal commission. Brown did not get the chance to build many houses, and his work at Claremont shows his eye to be assured and elegant, without any radical departures from the popular Palladian style. Credit should also be given to Henry Holland, Brown's son-in-law, who was responsible for the splendid interior decoration, some of which can still be

155

seen today. Sadly, Clive died before the house was finished and probably never lived there.

After three more owners, in 1816 the house and its park of 200 acres was bought by Parliament as a gift to the Prince Regent's daughter, Princess Charlotte, on her marriage to Prince Leopold of Saxe-Coburg. The couple loved the house and held many entertainments there, until the young princess tragically died giving birth to a stillborn son on 6 November 1817. Leopold never recovered, and lived on at Claremont, now a sad memorial to his beloved wife, until his investiture as King of Belgium in 1831. The young Queen Victoria often visited Claremont, and remembered it fondly as a wonderful place for children, with its beautiful gardens and lake where boating and picnics took place.

The house remained the property of the Royal Family through the beginning of this century, when Queen Victoria settled it on her youngest son, the Duke of Albany. During the 1914–18 war, the Duchess of Albany offered the house as an Officers' Convalescent Home. Owing to anti-German sentiment against the Albanys (their son, on instructions from the Queen, had succeeded to the Dukedom of Saxe-Coburg and Gotha before the war and hence had to become a German citizen), the house was confiscated after the war and reverted to private hands. In 1930, the Trustees of a Christian Science school for girls bought the house and thirty-seven acres (the estate having been divided up into lots), and by 1939 about eighty-five students were installed at Claremont.

Its history of German royal domesticity notwithstanding, Claremont found itself playing a role of great importance in the Second World War. In nearby Kingston was based one of the factories of Hawker Aircraft (the others were at Brooklands and Langley) where, by 1938, the fighter aeroplane known as the Hurricane was being produced as fast as it could be built. At the outbreak of war, the RAF had received about 500 Hurricanes from the Kingston and Brooklands works, and the prototypes of the Typhoon were already in production. Needless to say, these factories were prime German targets, and in early 1940 it was decided to remove the design office of Hawker Aircraft, under the direction of Sydney (later Sir Sydney) Camm, away from the central danger zone in Canbury Park Road, Kingston – to Claremont House.

'When I was fifteen I left school and immediately went to work "for the war effort", as we called it,' recalls Liane Keen. 'After a brief stint at a film studio which made animated cartoons for the services, I went to Hawker Aircraft.

'I was a tracer; there were about ten of us at Claremont and I was the youngest. We were given the original working drawings of sections of the

Hurricane, Typhoon and Tempest and we traced them onto thick blue coated paper from which blueprints could then be made. It was the greatest honour and thrill to be given a whole side elevation of a plane to trace; this would take three or four days to complete.

'I loved Claremont House and its grounds and have the happiest memories of whistling my way through the corridors and up and down that grand staircase. But when I was old enough I tried to join the WRNS or WAAFs because it was so much more glamorous. As civilians we had no uniforms, no extra clothing coupons, and above all, no prestige. It was a top-secret department of course, and the house was suitably remote. I had to cycle three miles every day to work. We had air raids every night, and you could set your watch by the hour the air raid warning went off. But one evening when I was on my way home after visiting a friend, the raid started early. I was at the point of no return. I pedalled madly but within moments anti-aircraft flak was falling all around me. I kept going, and got back winded but unhurt. My mother thought I might never come home.'

Claremont, unlike many country houses, was already adapted for use as an institution. But it commanded a dramatically lofty position, thanks to Capability Brown, making the most of the spectacular view. Moreover the building is faced with Portland stone, making it easily visible from the air. So for the duration of the war camouflage netting was draped over it, anchored with concrete blocks. Many of these blocks can still be seen in the grounds and now are used to prevent unauthorized car parking. Traces of green camouflage paint also remain on some of the roof stonework.

Like many requisitioned stately homes, remnants of Claremont's grand history were still in place, untouched by the school authorities. Even though all the royal possessions were removed when Claremont ceased to be royal property in 1922 (including the famous carpet Clive brought back from India for which the large room at the back – now the school library – was designed, measuring some sixty by eighty feet), beautiful damask wallcoverings, magnificent marble fireplaces, elaborate mouldings, gilt panelling, a tiny dumbwaiter, the occasional piece of antique furniture, were all still in evidence to remind the Hawker staff of what the house had been. The main drawing offices, where Hurricanes, Typhoons and Tempest aircraft were being developed, were on the ground floor, with eight or nine draughtsmen in each of the large sitting rooms. The ballroom was a canteen. (The catering staff found the dumbwaiter something of a challenge.)

'There was some excellent tapestry panelling and other features,' described Sir Frederick Page, one of the members of the Hawker team. 'Nothing was covered up. It provided a very pleasant atmosphere. But you must remember that most of the people working there were educated, skilled artists, who appreciated their surroundings.'

One of the house's features still intact after 150 years was a large and very elegant marble sunken bath, built for Lord Clive, apparently for medical rather than sybaritic reasons. This bath was requisitioned by the Hawker printing department to house printing machinery. 'We all thought it rather a waste,' observes Sir Frederick. 'We would have much preferred to have taken baths there with the appropriate female company.'

The occupants were, however, allowed free rein in the spectacular gardens which, although overgrown and neglected, provided a very pleasing place in which to wander. 'We used to have lunch in the gardens,' remembers Dennis Mason, another member of the team. 'You could really lose yourself, the rhododendrons were so overgrown.' Lunch may have sometimes led to other things, as Sir Frederick Page implies. 'It used to be customary to escort young ladies from the establishment through the park,' he says. 'The surroundings were very romantic, with the lake and the grotto.' There was also a folly or gazebo in the grounds, and at the back of the house a large swimming pool.

While bombs fell constantly around the areas of Kingston and Esher (Langley, Brooklands and the Canbury Park Road were all hit), Claremont remained safe from damage. Part of the grounds was used by the Army for training in grenade throwing, and signs of munitions dumping still occasionally surface, but again damage was minimal. Although the house is so exposed (there were rumours at one stage that it was used as a navigation fix by German aircraft), the closest Liane Keen remembers the house coming to harm was the day she watched a doodlebug from the windows of the tracers' office on the second floor at the front of the house. 'They were such evil-looking things, those pilotless bombs with flames streaming out of their tails,' she recalls. 'This one was headed straight for us and we watched it, paralysed with awe rather than fear. Within a few hundred feet of us the engine cut out. (It had run out of fuel and would fly without direction until it landed.) In a breathtaking moment the plane made a sudden curve upwards, flew over the house and detonated in a field a mile or so beyond it. Perhaps Claremont House, like so many beautiful houses in England at that time, had a guardian angel.'

After the war, the school, removed temporarily to Wales, was able to return, and over the years has expanded, become coeducational, and increased its property to 100 acres. The students still work in rooms decorated with museum-quality wallcoverings and panelling, and pass through corridors where once queens and princesses played. Royal portraits and porcelain collections are scatttered about the house, reminding the residents of its fascinating past. The adjoining overgrown gardens, including the lake, grotto and folly, which were part of the original Vanbrugh and Royal estates and once so popular as a wartime trysting spot, now belong to the National Trust. After an extensive programme of restoration, the garden reopened as the Claremont Landscape Garden in 1979, and now again offers the visitor the unique opportunity to view the work of some of England's best-known designers, Vanbrugh, Bridgeman, Kent and Brown.

Secret Operations
WOBURN ABBEY

*'You've no idea how strange it is when one lives
in a house like this to read about it in the
words of others who have also lived here.'*
– The Marchioness of Tavistock, 1987

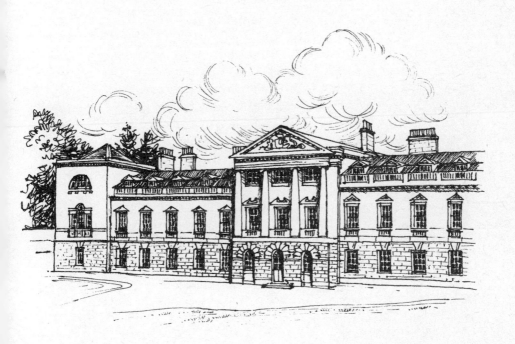

Woburn Abbey

WOBURN · BEDFORDSHIRE

WHEN THE SECOND World War broke out, Herbrand, the 11th Duke of Bedford, owner of Woburn Abbey, was seventy-nine years old, and in feeble condition. Two years earlier, his wife, Mary, known as 'The Flying Duchess' for her exploits as a daredevil solo pilot, had disappeared during a flight over the North Sea and was presumed dead, a tragedy which hastened the Duke's decline. Yet standards at Woburn were still maintained in the style of another age. The Duke's cousin, Conrad Russell, visiting Woburn shortly after the Flying Duchess's death, described the scene at breakfast: 'At nine minutes to nine we all assemble in the Canaletto Room. At nine the butler knocks loudly at the door, comes in and bawls, "Breakfast on the table, Your Grace." Herbrand says, "Well, shall we go into breakfast?" We all file in then. There are five men to wait on us, one for each. Everyone has their own tea or coffee pot. You help yourself to eggs and bacon. The butler takes your plate from you and carries it to your place. You walk behind him. It makes a little procession . . .'

Herbrand's grandson, the present Duke, who visited Woburn after being banished for some years, found his grandfather on the eve of the Second World War almost completely deaf and blind, living at Woburn with fifty indoor, and more than two hundred outdoor servants. According to the present Duke's eyewitness account, later published in a memoir, ten rooms were taken up by six nurses who watched over him in three shifts. 'At night the rooms were lit up with tremendously powerful bulbs, like a film studio, so that he could just distinguish his way by the differences of light and shade. He was more than a little senile, and longing to die.'

The Duke was not so senile, however, that he had not foreseen, like so many of his peers, that war was coming and that his house would be involved. In the First World War Woburn had been a military hospital, with the Flying Duchess a devoted nurse to some 2,000 patients who recuperated there. In early 1939 the Duke offered Woburn again to the Government, and this time the offer was taken up by Electra House, which housed the propaganda department at that time known as the Imperial Communications Advisory Committee under Sir Campbell Stuart, and which in 1940 became part of the Political Intelligence Division of the Foreign Office.

The accommodation for the staff of Electra House comprised two houses on the Woburn estate, the whole of the Henry Holland east wing, and the Riding School, Real Tennis Court, and Stables. No formal agreement was drawn up for the use of these buildings or compensation in case of damage (another 'gentleman's agreement', this time defended on grounds of the secret nature of the department in question), and the Duke requested no rent. Since at this time the main Abbey itself was not requisitioned, no particular arrangements were made for storage of treasures. (The Foreign Office provisionally listed the Abbey with the Office of Works as unavailable for requisitioning by other departments, or for the reception of evacuees.) The two State Coaches and Sedan Chair remained in the coach-house, while all other vehicles were removed. The Linnean Society (of which the Flying Duchess had been one of the first women members), and the Zoological Society, which had deposited certain cases in the tennis court at Woburn for safekeeping, were requested to oversee the removal of their cases to other quarters. (The Linnean Society sent a man to superintend the move; the Zoological Society said they did not mind who moved their possessions.) Partitions were put up for twenty-one cubicles (all made of asbestos — unthinkable today), and a list was made of the pictures and tapestries stored in the Riding School; beds were installed in the stables; blackout fabrics were ordered and installed; and the Intelligence department took up residence in September 1939.

The staff at the beginning consisted of seventy-five male, and forty-three female personnel. Sir Campbell Stuart brought his own domestic staff, while local help was commandeered for everyone else. Very soon, as in the case of so many country houses, the requisitioned accommodations proved too small.

By May 1940, Colonel Gordon, the Duke's Chief Agent, was reduced to writing in desperation to their local MP, Alan Lennox-Boyd, at Westminster:

'The Department is continually expanding and they are always anxious to take any empty house in the Park for their accommodation. They are continually threatening us with the use of their compulsory powers and even talk of occupying a part of the main Abbey. I have Campbell Stuart's written undertaking that he will not ask for any accommodation in the Abbey as long as the Duke is alive.' The present Duke records how his grandfather treated this problem. 'They asked at one point whether they could possibly take over one of the wings of the Abbey as overflow because they were so terribly crowded and had received a terse reply from my grandfather saying that they did not seem to appreciate that there was someone living in the house, although most of the hundred rooms must have been empty.'

Not only questions of accommodation reached the failing Duke's ears. The occupants on one occasion wished to try out an 'exceptionally strong wireless loudspeaker in the Park ... provided we do it at a time when the Duke is not likely to be about'. They also wanted to play football in the Park, and perhaps not surprisingly, to see the art collection in the Abbey. Most of these requests were granted, but the old Duke was not entirely *hors de combat*. He used to walk up and down beside a large cedar tree in the Park, and it was alleged that if anyone crossed an invisible line near the tree, the Duke would frighten the trespasser away. He may have been fierce, but he was also generous, offering them pheasants at Christmas, and allowing them to skate on the lake.

In August 1940, the 11th Duke died, leaving £4,651,371, on which death duties of £3,100,000 were imposed, which were still being paid off when the present Duke inherited the title in 1953. The 12th Duke was a well-known eccentric, with political views that allied him most unfortunately with Nazism. It was highly ironic that this man was now the owner of Woburn, where some of the most important anti-German propaganda was being disseminated. Not surprisingly, the new Duke's reputation as a security risk required him to stay away as much as possible from the Abbey (a requirement he happily discharged, being less than eager to take up the chaotic affairs of the estate he had inherited), and having sent his representative, Mrs Ada Osborne Samuel, to install herself at Woburn, he retired to the Russell shooting estate in Scotland, Cairnsmore.

Mrs Samuel, an old friend of the Duke and former keeper of a boarding-house, turned out to be a formidable administrator. She unceremoniously stripped poor Colonel Gordon of his authority. 'I shall be glad if you will leave the Government officials to me,' she wrote in October 1940. 'Any plans or information given to them must be given by me. It is perhaps unfortunate, but I am the official servant of the Duke here, and hope to do my duty. Therefore will you please respect this.' By the end of the year, Colonel Gordon was gone. Mrs Samuel was astute enough to realize that the lack of written agreement between the Government and the Abbey was to Woburn's disadvantage, and attempted to get things on a more formal footing. She also exerted her authority in other ways, taking the key to the Muniment Room, for instance, where documents of great historical value were stored, causing panic amongst the staff who feared the key had been stolen, and that if there was a fire nobody could get in. 'I take entire responsibility for my action,' she wrote in response to the outcry, 'as the Muniment Room is under my authority and control.' For the rest of the war, Mrs Samuel ruled unopposed, while the Duke remained in Scotland, returning only occasionally to Woburn to visit her. The present Duke returned to Woburn after his father's death eight years later to find Mrs Samuel firmly in the saddle, 'extremely grand in a large car with a chauffeur ... I could not bring myself to warm to her or invite her assistance.'

By the end of 1940, the PID, as the late Duke had feared, had moved into the Abbey itself. During this time, Sir Alec Martin, a representative of Christie's, had sorted out pictures and plate to be sold for death duties, and others to be sent to Cairnsmore for safekeeping. Several state rooms and the library were to be retained by the Woburn Estate trustees, into which were placed pictures and as much valuable furniture as could be stored there. 'The objection to the scheme is, of course, that the more valuables that are stored in one spot, the greater the loss would be if a bomb hit that particular spot,' observed one of the Woburn lawyers to the land agent. 'If the articles were distributed throughout the Abbey it would probably take several bombs to destroy them, but on the other hand they might suffer considerable damage at the hands of the Government department occupying the premises.'

This was precisely the dilemma faced by many country house-owners. In the event, Woburn was not bombed, and many of the treasures remained *in situ*. Perhaps too many, as a young woman of Anglo-French extraction who went to Woburn in 1941 was to find out. Jeanne Fawtier, who had been working with the Free French in London, was given a job at Woburn that year as an intelligence research assistant.

'A Packard limousine drove us out of London and off we went, destination unknown. When we got to this great house I got out of the car and went to the porter's lodge where I swore the Official Secrets Act. Only then was I allowed into the house.

'As country houses go, this one didn't strike me at the time as being one of the more handsome ones. Of course it was better in those days because the main house was still square. The East Wing had not been pulled down. It was not a warm house inside – no one loved it or cared for it. By this time the whole of the Abbey had been taken over, as well as the Tennis Court and Riding School.

I started in an office in the Henry Holland House, and then moved down to the Riding School, which had been partitioned to make little cubicles. The acoustics were non-existent. No privacy at all. There was a very nice man whose wife was in another department, and they had been married many, many years, and it was obviously rather a stormy marriage. They were always separating and making it up and he was always ringing her up suggesting meetings, and the entire office would hear all this. It didn't worry him in the slightest.

'I moved to the Canaletto Room during my second year there. There they were, all twenty-nine views of Venice or however many it was [twenty-two in fact], and it put me off Canaletto for a good twenty years. It didn't put me off Venice, only Canaletto. Later I saw some nice Canalettos of London which made me like him a bit more, but I always thought Guardi a much better painter. The major furniture had been removed from the room, but the carpet stayed. I was deeply shocked because it was a most beautiful Savonnerie carpet obviously made for the room, and all our desks and chairs were placed on top of it. Being Savonnerie, it was not the kind of carpet people were used to in England, and I don't think anybody realized how good a carpet it was.

'All the bedroms were turned into dormitories. I started off in a servants' bedroom which had six iron beds in it, but by chance a secretary in the administration (and therefore privileged) got given the housekeeper's room and she invited me to share it with her. The housekeeper's room was immediately opposite the Duchess's bathroom. In the summer this was very nice but in the winter it was horrible, because the Duchess's bath was very fine porcelain, which means it was freezing cold. A tin bath would have been much better. Also it was so huge one could never fill it up.

'Some people got to sleep in the Duke's bedroom, or some of the other grand rooms. In these rooms all the paintings had been removed so you had blank spaces to look at, revealing wonderfully new-looking wallpaper, the rest being very faded and old. At least those pictures were stored somewhere. I couldn't understand why the Russells didn't put more pictures away. Every day I would walk past that charming painting by a Dutchman of the then-Duchess of Bedford bare-bosomed, clad for a masque in a costume designed by Inigo Jones [Lucy, Countess of Bedford]. I loved it but kept thinking it should not have been hanging there.

'When I wanted to go to the loo, and if I had time, rather than go to the one closest to my office, I would go to the front of the house [the east wing] where there was a suite of quite small rooms which had been charmingly decorated in the Regency period. The loo itself was very early and absolutely gorgeous. You climbed up a couple of steps and the vessel was made of Wedgwood, with a highly-polished heavy rosewood seat. And because it was so far away, no one was ever there! All that is gone, it was part of the wing that was pulled down.

'After one's meagre lunch one would walk in the park where one might meet a variety of strange animals, but I never saw the herd of bisons. I remember trying to find the grotto with a friend. We finally discovered it. They were using it to store mattresses. It looked funny, this strange room with pillars and alcoves, studded with oyster shells, piled up with mattresses. I remember thinking it rather a damp place in which to keep them.

'At the back of the stables on Saturday night we had the Saturday Night Hop. It was all very democratic. The trouble was we were mostly women, so in order to get a mixed quota you had to invite the policemen, messengers and so on to join in. Sometimes this was quite fun because some old Ducal servants would come. One very elderly chap, who had been the Duke's chauffeur, introduced me to snuff.'

While Jeanne Fawtier spent her time evaluating documents (and carpets) in the Canaletto Room, some of the most secret work was being done on the estate, where broadcasters under the aegis of the Political Warfare Executive, as the Woburn outfit was now called, were waging what was called a 'black war' against Germany. In 1942 a secret radio station was built at Milton Bryan, and by 1943, waves of broadcasts were being transmitted from this station as though coming from within Europe, conveying messages which it was hoped would provoke an undercurrent of dissent and disillusion, leading to defection from Hitler and his cause. Designed to appeal to every level of European listener, pornography, crude language, pop music, jokes, were all used by these 'black' broadcasters to sow seeds of doubt and despair in the mind of the enemy. 'These chaps lived completely cut off from everyone,' Jeanne remembers, 'pretending to do clandestine radio in their country of origin. The atmosphere of unreality was quite extraordinary.

'I suppose Woburn was a perfectly good place in which to do hush-hush work, but one of the absurd things was that after about three years we got a message from the local Air Force people saying, "Do you chaps realize you've got WOBURN written in large letters all over your roof?" It was there for the benefit of the Flying Duchess, who was always trying to fly home in the fog.'

Woburn remained 'up for grabs' as the war proceeded. The park was requisitioned by the Air Ministry in February 1941. By the end of that year part of the park was also being used by the Ministry of Aircraft Production. The usual issues arose – trees to be felled, the 11th Duke's collection of wild animals, including the Père David's deer, to be removed, roads to be built, a hockey field to be created – several bureaucratic empires attempting to operate with an absentee owner and a dishevelled estate staff. By 1944 400 WRNS had taken up residence in the Abbey, the PIDs having moved back into the riding school. This was the state of affairs until the end of the war, when all the departments left. Then ensued the typical mopping-up period, with the Duke returning from Scotland to claim backdated rental of land, rates, compensation for damage, etc. Rather than move into the huge, exhausted Abbey, the Duke took up residence in the village. He never moved back.

The estate still owed staggering amounts of death duties, and the Duke thought of letting part of Woburn to a hospital to help repay these horrendous debts. But since he was only prepared to offer a few beds, there were no takers. Instead, he decided to demolish the east wing (which was riddled with dry rot), which included Henry Holland's Entrance Front, and the block containing the tennis court and riding school. Thus instead of retrenching, the Duke assumed huge architectural and contractors' bills for the saving of the Abbey. Unfortunately, the Duke and his advisers failed to acquire the proper building licences for these elaborate structural changes (very strict rules about building had been introduced after the war), and Mrs Samuel and a colleague were sent for trial for these improprieties. She was fined fifty pounds and the family company fined £5,000 with £300 costs – hardly a welcome sight on the mounting expenses ledger. After the demolition, the very expensive architect Sir Albert Richardson was hired to redesign the truncated wing and courtyard.

When the present Duke succeeded to the title in 1953, he returned to Woburn after thirteen years to find devastation. The east wing was a pile of rubble. There were still Nissen huts put up by the WRNS in the courtyard. The interior, as he described it, 'looked as if it belonged to a series of bankrupt auction rooms'. With superhuman effort on the part of the Duke, and with the support of his son, the Marquess of Tavistock, who now lives there with his family, Woburn was returned to its former position as a cornerstone of

Britain's national heritage, and its treasures, witness to some of the most crucial activities ever performed in time of war, now offer peacetime pleasure to succeeding generations of visitors.

Index